# MORE POWER TO THE SOVIETS

# THE INTERNATIONAL LIBRARY OF STUDIES IN COMMUNISM

**General Editor: Ronald J. Hill,**
*Trinity College, Dublin*

The International Library of Studies in Communism is an important new series covering all aspects of communism, but focusing principally on communism as a system of rule. At a time when the Stalinist form of socialism is undergoing reappraisal and modification in the leading communist-ruled countries, and newly emergent nations are being led along the communist path, the need to understand this phenomenon has never been greater.

The series is edited under the sponsorship of Lorton Hall, an independent charitable association which exists to promote the academic study of communism.

# MORE POWER TO THE SOVIETS

## The Democratic Revolution in the USSR

**Michael E. Urban**
**Auburn University**

Edward Elgar

Published by
Edward Elgar Publishing Limited
Gower House
Croft Road
Aldershot
Hants GU11 3HR
England

Gower Publishing Company
Old Post Road
Brookfield
Vermont 05036
USA


**British Library Cataloguing in Publication Data**

Urban, Michael E.
  More power to the Soviets: the democratic revolution in
  the USSR. – (The International library of studies in
  communism).
  1. Soviet Union. Political events, history
  I. Title II. Series
  320.947


Printed in Great Britain by
Billing & Sons Ltd, Worcester



ISBN   1  85278  330  3

# TABLE OF CONTENTS

# PREFACE

This book concerns the cardinal aspects of the democratic transformation of the Soviet polity: the transfer of power from the administrative organs of the party-state to elected legislatures; and the emergence of citizens' movements at the grassroots that would fill these legislatures with a popular content. Although these two aspects are tightly intertwined, the first refers primarily to reforms initiated 'from above' (that is, by the Gorbachev leadership) while the second, a response 'from below', represents a completely new dynamic in the political system whose appearance is nothing short of revolutionary. Indeed, a measure of its significance can be taken from the fact that whereas the reformers had stood in the forefront of the struggle for democracy at the outset of the transformation, they have been rather rapidly overtaken by self-organizing citizens who would press the struggle further. Ironically, Mikhail Gorbachev, whose commitment to democracy has been unprecedented among Soviet leaders, has more and more found himself in the role of attempting to limit and restrain those popular forces that his reform programme has summoned forth.

The time frame of this study is loosely bounded by the January (1987) Plenum of the Communist Party, on one end, and the close of the first session of the newly-elected Supreme Soviet (August 5, 1989), on the other. The focus, then, is on the first phase of political *perestroika*, extending from a general conception of democratization advanced at that Plenum by Gorbachev to its realization in the new Soviet parliament. But history rarely if ever occurs in such cleanly-sliced segments of time. The new has been gestated within the old in the same way that the completion of its initial stage of development already anticipates certain features of the stage that follows. Accordingly, I have attempted to situate the first phase of *perestroika* in the foreground by sketching the historical context from which it has emerged and by outlining those forces that have developed within it which seem to portend its future direction.

Chapter One introduces the basic problem that Gorbachev's political reforms have been designed to tackle—a system of moribund governmental institutions (soviets) whose absence in the real political life of the USSR has been concomitant with the capture of power by those occupying administrative positions in the party-state hierarchy. This interlocking directorate of officials had more and more become a governing class wielding power in its own interests and, often enough, in opposition to the directives issued by nominal superiors in the national leadership. Owing to their control of the apparatus of policy implementation, they have been able to thwart time and again the policy initiatives of the leadership and to escape responsibility for so doing. Increasingly, the national leadership found themselves presiding over a system of mismanagement, waste and corruption that they were seemingly helpless to correct.

The measures adopted by the Gorbachev leadership to solve this problem are presented in the remainder of Chapter One. They appear in the form of a series of Constitutional amendments and a new electoral law that are intended to transfer decision-making power from the party-state apparatus to elected legislatures (soviets) at all levels in the political system. Since the debates over, and formulation of, these reforms comprise the main topic in subsequent chapters, they are outlined here as a sort of reference point for the discussions that follow.

Chapter Two undertakes an analysis of the origins of the reforms. It recounts how the changes in Soviet political language introduced by Gorbachev have laid the foundation for an open discussion (initially within small circles of the intelligentsia, later among larger segments of the general public) of common problems, problems that seem immediately traceable to the irresponsible rule of the apparatus. Yet the strange symmetry of Gorbachev's reform coalition that includes both radical democrats on the left and conservative officials on the right has meant that unsteady compromises on the scope and pace of reform would be evident in every phase of the process. In order to ensure the backing of the powerful apparatus for their programme, reformers would offer concessions which would pare down the dimensions of democratization. Galled by the unsightly spectacle of such compromises, those on the left would later marshal their forces against them and thus renew the struggle for democracy.

The question of compromise is taken up in greater detail in Chapter Three. Here the discussion moves behind the scenes, as it were. It examines the work of those who composed the reform project, how they were entangled in the contradictions attendant on initiating democratization 'from above' while at the same time offering concrete assurances to the apparatus that the new political order whose framework they were drafting would be one in which its basic interests could be accommodated.

In Chapter Four, the Soviet public begins to enter the picture as the reform project is published along with an invitation to the citizenry to express their opinions on it. At this point the coalition of forces that had been backing reform unravels. The architects of the proposals, in concert with the apparatus, conduct a 'nationwide assessment' of the reform project that reaches the foreordained conclusion that the reforms enjoy the overwhelming support of Soviet society. Simultaneously, democratic forces emerge at the grassroots who register their opposition to the proposals, seeing them as a betrayal of the promised democratization. These forces gather strength during the ensuing national elections and score a number of remarkable victories at the polls that are discussed in Chapter Five.

The emergence of an active public in the USSR has represented the turning-point for *perestroika*. Within the newly-constituted national legislature, public demands have been forcefully voiced by a sizable minority of representatives who have gone into open opposition to the apparatus-dominated majority. Ironically, however, this democratic minority has tended more and more to set the legislative agenda and lead the way in formulating solutions to the problems besetting the country. Chapter Six, which discusses the first session of the Congress of People's Deputies and the Supreme Soviet, also examines how new policies developed at the national level for the republics and the localities are enabling the project of democratic government to go forward into its second and more radical stage.

Throughout the course of this study, it has been my good fortune to have received the informed counsel of a number of scholars, activists and public officials in the Soviet Union, many of whom I am happy to number among my friends. I would especially like to express my gratitude in this regard to: Georgii Barabashev, Vitalii Karpukhin, Vyacheslav Igrunov, Mikhail Forin, Mikhail Malyutin, Mikhail Schneider, Aleksei Lyubimov, Elena Makeeva, Vladimir Pribylovskii, Sergei Mitrokhin, Avgust Mishin, S. A. Avak'yan, A. V. Luk'yanchikov, E. I. Korenevskaya, Virgilius Chepaitis, Tomas Urba, Yurii Feofanov, Oleg Shcherbakov, Elena Zelinskaya, V. D. Pertsik,

Vladimir Stratanovich, V. Pakalniskis, Valerii Fadeev, Sergei Kuz'michev, A. T. Leizerov, A. N. Kramnik and M. F. Chudakov.

Among those Western scholars whose criticisms and suggestions have greatly benefitted my efforts, I wish to thank in particular Eugene Huskey, Ronald Hill, Brendan Kiernan, Thomas Remington, Blair Ruble and Stephen White.

Finally, this book would not have been possible without the financial support provided by the International Research and Exchanges Board, the National Endowment for the Humanities and the University of Illinois' Slavic Research Summer Laboratory, and the moral support supplied by my wife, Veronica, and children, Emily and George.

# 1. INTRODUCTION: THE PROBLEM AND THE SOLUTION

At its extraordinary session of 29 November to 1 December 1988, the Supreme Soviet of the USSR adopted a series of amendments to the Soviet Constitution and a new Law on Elections that radically reconstructed the USSR's governmental institutions and opened the door for the country's first competitive nationwide elections. The Soviet Union thus embarked on the road to democracy, a long road, to be sure, and one that in this particular case seems to have more than its share of confusing twists and turns. In order to navigate our way we require at least two points of reference to keep our discussion on course. The first involves the matter of background or context. Here we are concerned to sketch the dimensions of the problem that the Gorbachev leadership inherited in the area of government and politics, one that it has attempted to solve by means of its policy of 'democratization'. In short, the problem was that a system of ostensibly popular institutions, the soviets, had been thoroughly captured by the administrative apparatus of the Communist Party and, in the process, completely eviscerated as institutions of government.

The second point of reference is the 'solution' that the Gorbachev leadership has developed to remedy the problem. Here, we focus our attention on the main provisions of the Constitutional amendments and Law on Elections that the Supreme Soviet adopted at its extraordinary session. Since the remainder of this book is concerned to show how these legislative changes came about and to analyze the new political system that has emerged in the USSR in the wake of their adoption, we refrain at this point from commenting on the legislation in question, except to note in a few instances some differences that exist between its final version and the initial drafts submitted to the Soviet public for comment some one month prior to ratification.

## THE PROBLEM

Among the officially established 'truths' promulgated by the Soviet regime during the first 70 years of its existence, none surpassed the outright mendacity that it reserved for the system of soviets. At issue here was not only the regime's penchant for prevarication, for it had amply demonstrated its willingness to alter or abolish the facts pertaining to any phenomenon in order to absolve itself of responsibility for what had gone wrong or, better, to cover itself with accolades for what had allegedly gone right. Of equal if not greater moment in this regard was the fact that the hypocrisy displayed by the regime toward the soviets corrupted the very identity that the regime claimed for itself. For it had never ceased to refer to its domain as 'the country of soviets' where lived the *Soviet* people, and always availed itself of this same identity marker in speaking about the order that it had created ('our Soviet way of life', 'the new Soviet man', and so forth), even while it had eviscerated the soviets themselves, converting them into lifeless assemblies that resembled governmental institutions in the way that zombies might resemble the living.

Soviets (literally, 'councils') first appeared in Russia during the aborted Revolution of 1905. They emerged initially as strike committees composed of workers' representatives who sought to coordinate industrial actions on their respective territories. Quickly, however, they began to challenge the authority of the Tsarist state on political matters and, consequently, took on the character of incipient governments. Although crushed in the course of the restoration of Tsarist authority, they re-emerged during the early days of the Russian Revolution of 1917 and rapidly began to concentrate government powers into their own hands. At the Second All-Russian Congress of Soviets of Workers' and Soldiers' Deputies convened in the autumn of 1917, delegates representing soviets from across Russia adopted the Bolshevik platform of taking power from the Provisional Government that had succeeded the Tsar but which had failed to consolidate its own authority and had lost most of the limited popular support that it had earlier enjoyed. Proclaimed the October Revolution: 'All power to the soviets!'

Although the modern Soviet Union was inaugurated by this seizure of political power by the soviets, it was not long before these soviets themselves had receded into the background. Part of the reason for this lay in their own methods of organization and work. As early as 1918, strong criticisms from the Revolution's rank-and-file were appearing to the effect that inside the soviets bureaucratic forms of organization were replacing democratic ones, and that soviets were severing their heretofore vital connections with the population by closing their meetings to the public and failing to inform the citizenry about the work of their own government.[1] A second and more important factor accounting for the short lifespan of soviets as autonomous institutions of government, however, was the restrictive policies pursued by the Communist Party.

The Communist leadership was not adverse to employing coercive measures against its political opponents within the soviets, 'correcting, where necessary, the results of the ballot box by force'.[2] But at its Eighth Congress in 1919, the Communist Party developed a somewhat more sophisticated approach to the question that proved capable of killing the problems of opposition parties and (potentially, if not actually) unreliable soviets with the same organizational stone. The Congress resolved, on the one hand, that each soviet would be internally directed by a 'guiding nucleus' of Communist Party members within it and, on the other, that these guiding nuclei would themselves be directed by a newly-formed apparatus of the Communist Party. As a result, all parties save the Communists were expelled from the soviets by 1922,[3] and by the following year the party apparatus was well on its way to exercising complete dominion over the soviets by vetting candidates for office and installing those whom it had selected in leading posts.[4] These practices transpired through the institution of the *nomenklatura*, appointments lists that party organizations use to staff all positions of import with those approved by the narrow circles of party functionaries.

As Soviet history entered its Stalinist epoch, a measure of the relevance that remained for soviets as governmental institutions can be taken from the fact that they had largely dispensed with the formality of holding meetings, even for ceremonial purposes.[5] Power was exercised in varying degrees by the administrative triumvirate of the Stalin system—the secret police, the centralized state ministries and the party

apparatus—while the soviets simply lapsed into political irrelevance.
Efforts to revive them after Stalin's death yielded no more than cosmetic
improvements[6] until the Gorbachev leadership unveiled its programme
for political *perestroika* in 1988.

## THE SOLUTION

Political *perestroika* has been institutionalized by the Constitutional
amendments and Law on Elections adopted for the expressed purpose
of transforming soviets into authentic institutions of popular government. These measures comprise the second of our reference points.
Therefore, our concern here is to outline the important changes that they
have introduced into the organizational structure of Soviet government.
Accordingly, our discussion addresses the questions of how the new
legislative bodies are composed, the formal powers that have been
awarded to them, and the legislative changes that have been introduced
in the areas of sub-national governments and the courts.

*Elections to the Congress of People's Deputies.* The amendment to
Article 108 of the Soviet Constitution of 1977 has established a new
legislative body, the Congress of People's Deputies, as 'the supreme
organ of state power in the USSR'. In form, the new Congress very
much resembles the old Supreme Soviet. It sits for five years but,
ordinarily, convenes for only a few days out of each. It can be called
into special session, however, by a petition of one-fifth of its members.[7]
It has retained the old electoral arrangement whereby 750 deputies are
elected in 'territorial districts' with equal numbers of eligible voters and
750 are elected in 'national-territorial districts', of which there are 32
in each of the fifteen union republics of the USSR, and eleven and five,
respectively, in the smaller national subdivisions—autonomous
republics and autonomous regions—that exist within some of the larger
union republics. To these 1,500 deputies (elected by the citizens according to principles of representation based on either population or
national affiliation) is added another contingent of 750 who are selected
directly by public organizations, thus enlarging the 'supreme organ of
power' to 2,250 members and establishing a new principle of representation based on social activity[8] (see Fig.).

**Figure. Organizational Structure of the Government of the USSR**

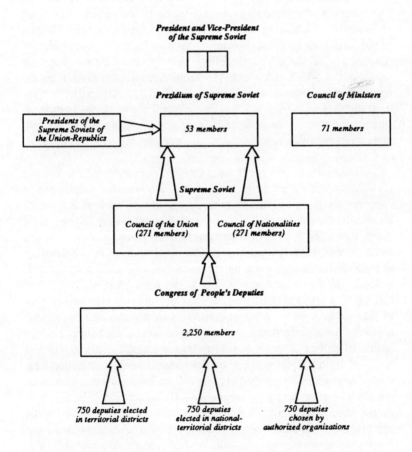

The new Law on Elections continues the longstanding practice whereby the 'preparation and conduct' of elections are duties entrusted to electoral commissions. These electoral commissions are formed in each territorial or national-territorial district by their respective soviets on the basis of nominations that have been submitted by labour collectives, public organizations or meetings of voters in their places of residence. They are also formed in each of the public organizations at the national level that has the right to name deputies to the Congress. Their work is supervised by a Central Electoral Commission, composed of 35 members who have been nominated by either the executive bodies of public organizations at the national level or by the 'higher organs of state power of the union republics', and approved by the Supreme Soviet of the USSR. The Central Electoral Commission establishes the boundaries of the single-member territorial and national-territorial electoral districts, disburses funds to the electoral commissions in order to finance the cost of the candidates' campaigns and the election itself, and carries out other tasks related to the election, registration and recall of deputies.

Nominations to the 1,500 seats that are popularly elected are put forward through four distinct channels: meetings of employees in factories, collective or state farms, or institutions such as schools or hospitals; the executive bodies of social organizations at any level below the national; meetings of citizens in their places of residence; and assemblies of military personnel in their respective units. Nominations in each district are open and unlimited, but no individual may serve as a deputy to more than two soviets at the same time and executive officials of a given soviet, excluding the chief, may not serve as deputies to that same soviet. When more than two nominations have been advanced in a given district, the electoral commission there has the option of calling a 'pre-electoral district meeting'. This meeting is attended by an equal number of delegates from labour collectives, voters' assemblies in residential areas and military units that have been invited to participate by the local electoral commission. Those whose names have been placed in nomination have the right to address the pre-electoral district meeting and to answer questions from the delegates. By majority vote—either openly or secretly, according to the rule adopted by those in attendance—the pre-electoral district meeting decides which names to register as candidates and enter on the ballot. For candidates running in the territorial and national-territorial districts, voting occurs by striking off the name(s) of that (those) candidate(s) that the voter does not prefer. Voting is by secret ballot only. The winning candidate is then the one whose name has been struck off the least number of times, providing that over half of the eligible voters in the district have participated in the balloting and that this candidate's name was not crossed off by 50 per cent or more of those voting. When more than two candidates have competed and none has received a majority of votes, a runoff election is subsequently held between the top two vote-getters. In those cases in which one or two candidates have stood for a seat and neither has received a majority of the votes cast, or those in which voter participation fell below the 50 per cent mark, new elections are required.

Elections within those public organizations with the right to select deputies follow a similar pattern. Nominations are submitted by the constituent units of a given public organization to a plenary session of its national committee, members of which also have the right to introduce other nominations. The plenary session then composes a list of candidates either equal to or greater than the number of seats allotted to the organization. This list is then voted on at a subsequent meeting of either the national committee (in which might participate 'representatives of other electoral organs of this organization') or a full congress or conference of the organization itself. Those candidates whose names have been struck from the list the least number of times are named deputies in proportion to the number of seats to be filled by the organization, assuming that none of these had his name crossed off the list by half or more of those voting. Should the organization fail to fill its quota of deputies owing to such cross-offs, new nominations and elections are held to fill the vacancies.

*Functions of the Congress.* The Congress is empowered to carry out two basic functions. The first pertains to the exercise of its own authority in such areas as amending the Constitution (by two-thirds vote), defining the external boundaries of the USSR or those of its union republics, 'determining the basic directions of the foreign and domestic policies of the USSR', adopting the state budget and economic plan, reviewing (and either ratifying or rescinding) the laws and acts of the national government,[9] and initiating national referenda. Its second function is to constitute the various bodies that conduct the business of government on a full-time basis. To this end, the Congress elects by

secret ballot from among its members a Supreme Soviet, a President
and Vice-President of the Supreme Soviet and the Committee of Constitutional Oversight. It also confirms the appointment of the Chairperson of the Council of Ministers, the Chairperson of the Committee of
People's Control, the President of the Supreme Court, the Procurator
General and the Chief Arbiter of the USSR.

*The Supreme Soviet.* The 542 deputies elected to the Supreme Soviet
convene twice annually in sessions of three to four months' duration.
From year to year, one-fifth of the membership is replaced by other
deputies elected at the annual sessions of the Congress. The deputies
on the Supreme Soviet are equally divided into two chambers, the
Council of the Union and the Council of Nationalities. Each chamber
elects its own president and its own standing commissions.

The Supreme Soviet functions as the main legislative body in the
USSR. This is illustrated, firstly, by its powers of appointment. In
addition to confirming the appointments to the Council of Ministers and
electing the remaining members of the Committee of People's Control,
the Supreme Court, the Procuracy and the Collegium of State Arbitration, it appoints and dismisses the High Command of the Armed Forces
and approves the composition of the Military Council. Secondly, this
function is reflected directly in its legislative authority. According to
the amendment to Article 113 of the Constitution, the Supreme Soviet
is required 'to guarantee the uniformity of the legislation in effect on
all the territories of the USSR [and] to establish the basic legislation for
the USSR and the union republics.' It is further empowered 'to interpret
the laws of the USSR, ... to ratify and renounce international agreements ... to regulate property relations, the administrative organs of the
national economy ... the budget and finance systems, wages, taxes,
environmental protection, the use of natural resources, the Constitutional rights, freedoms and obligations of the citizenry and also other
matters'. Of particular importance in this regard is the Supreme
Soviet's responsibility in military and security affairs. While in session, it alone has the power to declare war, to order a partial or general
mobilization, and to commit Soviet troops to foreign soil.

Draft legislation can be submitted to either chamber of the Supreme
Soviet by the deputies themselves, the Prezidium or the President of the
Supreme Soviet, the Committee of Constitutional Oversight, the Coun-
cil of Ministers, the executive organs of public organizations and others.

These drafts would ordinarily be considered initially by the relevant standing committees or commissions in either or both of the chambers and then entered into the legislative agenda set by the Prezidium. In addition to adopting its own legislation, the Supreme Soviet has the power to revise or annul laws or executive degrees issuing from its President, Prezidium, the Council of Ministers of the USSR or the councils of ministers of the union republics. Decisions are carried by a majority in each chamber, with provision for the resolution of differences by means of a commission composed of members from each chamber, a joint sitting of both chambers or a submission of the question to the Congress when agreement between the chambers has not been reached.

*The Prezidium.* The Prezidium of the Supreme Soviet is the main organ for coordinating the various aspects of the legislative process. It is composed of the President, Vice-President and fifteen deputy presidents of the Supreme Soviet, the presidents of both chambers and chairpersons of the standing committees of the Supreme Soviet, the presidents of the supreme soviets of the union republics and Chairperson of the Committee of People's Control. It organizes the work of the Congress, the Supreme Soviet and its standing committees, and has the power to issue its own decrees and to conduct national referenda on questions designated by the Congress. The Prezidium accredits and dismisses foreign diplomats and can declare war, order mobilizations and commit troops abroad when the Supreme Soviet is not in session. It also exercises principal authority in the area of internal security with the power to declare martial law or a state of emergency for the entire country, or enact the same for particular localities in consultation with the prezidium of the supreme soviet of the relevant union republic.[11]

*The President and Vice-President.* The President of the Supreme Soviet is the head of state and, effectively, the commander-in-chief of the armed forces of the USSR. He is elected by the Congress for a five-year term of office, limited to serving no more than two consecutive terms, and can be removed by the Congress at any time. The President plays the principal role in the legislative process. He delivers policy reports to the Congress and the Supreme Soviet that outline his legislative agenda and 'exercises overall leadership in preparing the issues to be submitted to the consideration' of these bodies.

The President is the initiator of all appointments to the government's most important posts. He nominates the Vice-President and members of the Committee of Constitutional Oversight who are elected by the Congress, as well as a number of high officials who are elected by the Supreme Soviet. This latter group includes the Chairperson of the Council of Ministers, the Chairperson of the Committee of People's Control, the President of the Supreme Court, the Procurator General, and the Chief State Arbiter, all of whose elections are subsequently confirmed by the Congress.

It is not clear, however, what inherent powers reside in the office of the President. The amendment to Article 121 of the Constitution mentions that the President 'issues directives' (*izdaet rasporyazheniya*) which are presumably of lesser moment than the 'decrees' and 'resolutions' (*ukazy* and *postanovleniya*) that the Prezidium is empowered to enact. But the language of the amendment does not specify the nature of these 'directives', and it is not possible to ascertain at this point whether 'directives' represent authoritative acts autonomously issued by the President or whether they refer to ancillary actions that he undertakes in order to implement a law passed by the Congress or the Supreme Soviet or a decree adopted by the Prezidium.[12]

*The Committee of Constitutional Oversight.* Legislation that is under the consideration of the Congress or the Supreme Soviet may be reviewed by a newly-established Committee of Constitutional Oversight should questions of constitutionality arise. This Committee is composed of 23 members,[13] none of whom is either a deputy or a holder of a high state office, who serve for terms of ten years. It acts on its own initiative or on requests from the Congress, either chamber or any of the standing committees of the Supreme Soviet, the President or Prezidium of the Supreme Soviet, the Council of Ministers or congresses of people's deputies in any of the union republics. It has the power to suspend temporarily the force of laws that it believes violate the Constitution or that of executive decrees that it holds to be inconsistent with either the Constitution or laws of the country. It transmits its opinions to those bodies that originally passed the law or issued the decree for their reconsideration, but cannot itself annul the law or decree in question.

*Government at the Republic and Local Levels.* The Constitutional amendments adopted on 1 December say little about sub-national government in the USSR, probably because of the fact that other reform legislation is being drafted that addresses the rights of the union republics and the powers of local soviets. Accordingly, only a sketchy statement appears in the amendment to Article 137 which establishes congresses of people's deputies in all of the union republics as their highest organs of state power and leaves to the respective constitutions of the union republics the task of specifying the scope and nature of their own congresses.[14] The amendment to Article 138 creates in each republic analogues to the legislative institutions established at the national level: a supreme soviet, responsible to its corresponding congress, that functions as a 'continuously acting legislative, managing (*rasporyaditel'nyi*) and monitoring (*kontrol'nyi*) organ of state power'; a prezidium of the supreme soviet; and a president of the supreme soviet who is also responsible to the congress. However, it assigns to the constitutions of the union republics the job of defining the authority of each of these institutions.

With respect to local soviets, including in that category those at the district, city and regional levels, an amendment to Article 149 requires that they form prezidiums headed by their respective presidents. Forthcoming legislation in this area is expected to elaborate on the composition of these bodies and on their relations to the executive committees of their corresponding soviets.

*Courts.* The Constitutional amendments adopted by the Supreme Soviet have introduced only two changes of any significance into the court system of the USSR. The first involves a modification of Article 152 such that judges at the district, city and regional levels are elected by soviets one level above them in the governmental hierarchy instead of by the corresponding soviet as had previously been the case.[15] This new arrangement for selecting judges is expected to increase the independence of the courts, as we see below. The second addresses the same issue of judicial independence by adding some teeth to Article 155. Appended now to this article is the provision that 'any sort of interference with the activities of judges and people's assessors regarding the dispensing of justice is impermissible and entails responsibility before the law'. Taken together, these amendments are intended to reduce, if not eliminate, political influence in the judicial process,

enabling courts to uphold the law, dispense justice uniformly and
contribute, thereby, to the establishment of a government of law in the
Soviet Union.

## NOTES

1. Alexander Rabinowitch, 'The Evolution of Local Soviets in Petrograd, November
   1917-June 1918: The Case of the First City District Soviet', *Slavic Review*,
   Vol. 46 (Spring, 1989), pp. 33-34.
2. Leonard Schapiro, *The Government and Politics of the Soviet Union* (3rd. ed.;
   London: Hutchinson and Co., 1968), p. 44.
3. Merle Fainsod, *How Russia is Ruled* (Rev. ed.; Cambridge, MA: Harvard University Press, 1967), pp. 135-137.
4. Leonard Schapiro, *The Communist Party of the Soviet Union* (New York: Vintage
   Books, 1960), pp. 243-246, 321-322.
5. A. I. Lepeshkin, *Sovety—vlast' trudyashchikhsya, 1971-1936* (Moscow:
   Yuridicheskaya literatura, 1966); *Sovety—vlast' trudyashchikhsya, 1936-
   1967* (Moscow: Yuridicheskaya literatura, 1967).
6. *Inter alia*, David D. Cattell, *Leningrad: A Case History of Soviet Urban Government* (New York: Praeger, 1968); William Taubman, *Governing Soviet
   Cities* (New York: Praeger, 1973); Michael E. Urban, 'Information and Participation in Soviet Local Government', *Journal of Politics*, Vol. 44 (Feb.,
   1982), pp. 64-85.
7. Article 110 awards the right to initiate such a petition to 'the Supreme Soviet of
   the USSR ... one of the chambers of the Supreme Soviet of the USSR, the
   Prezidium of the Supreme Soviet of the USSR, the President of the Supreme
   Soviet of the USSR [or]... a union republic in the person of its higher organ
   of state power.'
8. The new Law on Elections lists the public organizations eligible to send representatives to the Congress and apportions seats among them as follows: 100
   seats apiece for the Communist Party, the trade unions, and cooperative organizations and societies; 75 seats apiece for the League of Communist
   Youth (Komsomol), women's councils and the Committee of Soviet
   Women, veterans of war and labour, societies of scientists, engineers, inventors and rationalizers of production, creative unions (such as writers and ar-
   tists). The remaining 75 seats are divided among a number of other societies
   in the areas of culture and sport, as well as the Red Cross, the Red Crescent,
   and the Soviet Committee in Defence of Peace.
9. Deleted in the final version of the amendment was the provision whereby the Congress could repeal legislation enacted by any of the union republics if, in its
   view, such legislation did not correspond to the Constitution of the USSR.
10. The number of deputies on the Supreme Soviet was increased by about 120 over
    that specified in the initial draft of the amendment to Article 111 of the Con-
    stitution. The increase resulted mainly from raising the number of deputies
    from each union republic from seven to eleven and then adding an equal in-
    crement to the contingent of deputies from territorial districts.
11. The provision calling for consultation with the prezidium of that union republic af-
    fected by a localized declaration of martial law or state of emergency was
    added to the final draft of the amendment.

12. Inasmuch as the initial draft of this amendment contained a related provision (whereby the President 'exercises other powers granted him by the Constitution and laws of the USSR') that was removed from the final version, the second interpretation may be the more accurate one.
13. The final version of this amendment increased the size of the Committee of Constitutional Oversight from 15 (as specified in the initial draft) to 23 and introduced the requirement that this number must include 'representatives from each union republic.'
14. Two paragraphs included in the initial draft of this amendment that enumerated the powers and functions of the republic-level congresses were stricken from the final version. The same is true of the amendment to Article 143 which establishes congresses of people's deputies in all of the autonomous republics.
15. This represents a change both from the arrangement prescribed by the Constitution of 1977 and from that contained in the initial draft of this amendment.

# 2. TO THE NINETEENTH PARTY CONFERENCE

## THE OFFICIAL DISCOURSE AS IMPEDIMENT TO COMMUNICATION

Before they decided to tackle the problem of a governmental system that was manifestly ineffective as well as undemocratic, the Soviet authorities spent some thirty years talking about the issue. Publicly, at least, this talking went on within the constraints associated with the official doctrines of the Communist Party that were extant in those years. As such, a particular way of discussing governmental institutions—a discourse on soviets—came into being. Like any discourse that we might consider, it amounted to a set of shared meanings, usually latent but no less present, that served to constitute a group of individuals as a community of speakers. Individual utterances or narratives would be immediately intelligible to others in the community because these would refer back to, and draw on, the ensemble of shared meanings available to each party through his participation in the discourse.

This concept of discourse enables us to grasp the fact that communication depends upon the assumptions and background understandings present within a given community of speakers. Participation in a discourse engenders a sense of mutual understanding, the feeling that 'we are all speaking the same language'. Moreover, discourse enables us to appropriate, and comment on, the world in a particular way. In the field of organized sport, for instance, the discourse would highlight such things as, say, 'fairplay' (rather than 'charity') toward opponents and 'teamwork' (rather than 'divine providence') as a condition for success.

With respect to the discourse on soviets, it is important to remember that its central elements were defined by the political authorities and that these definitions were themselves backed by coercive power.

15

Communication, as a result, became excessively constrained and distorted. The official discourse not only marked off the limits of what could be communicated, it also prescribed the use of certain forms for addressing all questions pertaining to the status of soviets in the system, their proper role and the problems connected with it. In order to take part in the public discussion on governmental institutions and speak to the questions of what was wrong with the way in which soviets were performing, what remedies might be available and so forth, one was obliged to adopt the language of the official discourse on the soviets and remain within its narrow confines. In so doing, one was equally obliged to reiterate the established 'truths' (however preposterous) that characterized the soviets as the most democratic institutions of government in the world, ceaselessly labouring on behalf of the population's welfare under the infallible guidance of the Communist Party. The actual structures of power could not be called into question and it was, of course, impossible to suggest publicly that the discourse itself was in any way mistaken or inadequate. To address the issues associated with the role of soviets in the political system, therefore, was to speak through the categories provided by the official discourse. To speak through such categories, in turn, meant that at the outset the speaker would misstate everything concerned with the practical affairs of the soviets, for reports about events in the world would surely contradict the 'truths' enshrined in the official discourse. Although it may have been painfully clear that soviets were both undemocratic and impotent, the official discourse prescribed that all communication about soviets proceed from the 'truth' that inverted what was blatantly obvious in this respect. Communication could only be oriented to a 'further perfection' of this best-of-all-possible-worlds. It could not analyze this world from the standpoint of actual political processes themselves. As a consequence, a discourse that presented itself as a solution to the problem of governmental institutions became, in fact, another part of the problem.

A series of legislative acts, party resolutions and government decrees that were ostensibly designed to improve the performance of soviets illustrate quite well the inability of this discourse to engage practical problems and initiate instrumental action aimed at solving them.[1] Soviets, these 'reform' initiatives announced, must become the real masters of the territories which they govern. They must ensure the harmonious development of their respective territories, upgrade the services that they provide to the population, respond to the expressed needs of the citizens and take measures to involve the public more fully in the affairs of government. Without actually addressing the matter of why soviets have had a disappointing record in all of these areas and how the existing structure of incentives has led to some outcomes (problems) and not others (solutions), these reforms declared that *all* should be changed, *all* should be improved. Not surprisingly, the practical results of the measures officially announced and reiterated over a period of some thirty years were effectively nil.[2]

Here, an interesting question poses itself: How can we explain the repeated applications of a remedy that had shown itself time and again to be useless? This question in the context of yesterday's official discourse on the soviets has two answers. The first of these I have already elaborated elsewhere by noting that in fact the remedy was working all along, albeit not on the level of social practice.[3] Although the surface indications of the reform legislation concerning the soviets, or those sounded in, say, a major speech by the party leader on this topic, might appear to signal that the legislation or the speech in question was indeed about the world of practical affairs, a closer examination of the *structure* of these forms of communication would show otherwise.

Approaching the matter from the perspective of semiotics, it is possible to isolate two basic dimensions in the structure of discourse, a practical one that points to the outer world of social action and a mythic (or noological) dimension that invests the discourse with meaning, significance and value for those participating in it.[4] When viewing the old official discourse on the soviets in this way, it becomes clear that the practical dimension had been completely eclipsed by the mythic one. In this respect, the discourse appears as an analogue to the traditional Russian folktale wherein the vexed contradictions of life and the intolerable conditions of social existence are transformed in the movement of the tale into a system of symbols that turn contradiction into harmony, afford comfort to those listening and counsel patience to those who would endure.[5] Like the folktale, however, the meaning and function of the reform legislation concerning the soviets depended on the existence of a problem that it would not address in practical terms. The problem, then, was mythologized but not changed. As such, the legislation, decrees and so on could be regularly repeated, just as the tale could be endlessly retold. In either case, the actual conditions of social life that had set the discourse in motion remained outside the scope of the discourse itself.

The second answer to our question has become clear once the old discourse on the soviets was overthrown and replaced by a new one that has privileged the practical dimension over the mythic one. It had, in fact, existed for many years on the margins of the official political language as a set of concerns shared by many Soviet scholars and officials. It appeared in two forms. The more robust of these were face-to-face oral discussions in small groups. In this context, practical ideas could be developed in considerable depth but, since the circle of participants in any given case was necessarily narrow, these discussions were essentially private affairs. They lacked a medium for reaching a wider audience, one that could not only participate in the discussion but act on it in the world.

The second form taken by this alternative discourse might be described as a sort of clandestine guerilla warfare on the terrain of written communication. It amounted to limited incursions into the strongholds of the official mythology in the area of the soviets and appeared in two modes. The first of these emphasized the empirical. Here the writer would pay homage to the official discourse by employing its categories and celebrating its escatology, while he simultaneously subverted them by introducing his reader to the results of empirical investigations which showed that in reality soviets were but pathetic representations of the Herculean institutions of popular sovereignty that inhabited the mythic world portrayed in the official discourse.[6] This use of the code against the code, as it were, had the capacity to subvert but not to overturn the established 'truths' about soviets. It could document the gaps between fact and fiction, but could not discuss the reason(s) for the gaps themselves, for such would require the writer to analyze things from a perspective outside of the prescribed mode of communication, an activity that would turn clandestine warfare into open struggle and thereby invite retaliation from officialdom and censor alike.

The other mode of written communication that established a niche for itself on the apron of the official language consisted of the reform proposals of leading scholars that appeared in conventional books and articles. It attacked the established discourse in another, albeit equally indirect, way. Rather than overwhelming the outposts of established truth with a mass of data, its tactics were to juxtapose another conception, another way of organizing and acting, to the conventional methods of conducting soviet work.[7] In so doing, it invited the reader to imagine an alternative to the present state of affairs. If the empirical studies showed that things were not what they pretended to be, this approach went further in certain respects by asking that some of the pretences be dropped in favour of novel conceptions that promised improvements at the level of social practice.

We might, then, view these two modes of internal subversion as complementing one another; one publicized the fact that the established discourse did not correspond to events in the world, while the other suggested that this discourse incorporate some new elements and discard some old ones. At the same time, however, each was a severely restricted form of communication. For whether a given narrative challenged the empirical validity of official truths or proposed practical alternatives to the realization of that which the official truths proclaimed —effective, democratic government—in neither instance was it possible to carry out an analysis of the problem itself in terms of those concrete social relations that rendered soviets ineffective and undemocratic institutions. In order to do so, the official discourse would have to be dropped; yet upholding it was the price that one paid for admission to the theatre of public (written) discussion. A practical language was therefore blocked by the established discourse. Until this discourse was either altered or abolished, those trapped within it could snipe at problems but were unable to mount a full-scale assault on them.

## *PERESTROIKA* AS A RESTRUCTURING OF POLITICAL LANGUAGE

The accession of Mikhail Gorbachev to the post of General Secretary of the Communist Party in March 1985 fundamentally changed this situation. His policy of *perestroika*, or 'restructuring', was initially expressed as a restructuring of the language of politics itself. That is, in order to effect changes in the world of social practice, a change was first required in the language that actors in the world could employ to describe, analyze and understand it. Early in his tenure as General Secretary, Gorbachev introduced such a change. Although there was little in the surface content of his narrative that would at this time distinguish Gorbachev's rhetoric from that of his predecessors—he was not, as yet, speaking of political pluralism or democracy—the structure of his discourse was radically different.[8] The old discourse raised social problems only to bury them, calling their names in order to sing them to sleep. It was both closed to reports from the world of practice and unable to address that world. Gorbachev restructured this discourse. Firstly, he opened a space within it for uncertainty and doubt. Consequently, the leader, the party, history or whichever figure the old discourse employed to issue authoritative proclamations on how to apprehend the social world simply disappeared. Gorbachev was, of course, himself speaking with the authority of his position behind him. But he was using that authority in a radically new way, saying, in effect, 'I don't know, I'm not sure.' Secondly, this aspect of the structure of his discourse opened the way for practical communication with and among others. It immediately implied the questions: What do you think? What should we do? Finally, admitting the other (society) to a dialogue meant that truth claims could no longer be redeemed simply by recourse to the truths enshrined in the official mythology. If communication within the context of the discourse introduced by Gorbachev was to avoid collapsing into nonsense, then truth must be validated on the level of practice, the only criterion remaining once doubt and dialogue had taken the place of authoritative pronouncements. Since society was thereby included in the formulation of society's project, Gorbachev had in fact introduced the idea of democracy—and the lack of it—into the field of officially sanctioned political speech without having uttered the word himself.

For those who had kept alive the idea of genuine reform in the institution of the soviets during the long years of 'stagnation', the restructuring of political language effected by Gorbachev meant that ideas incubated in private discussion could now expect to find a place in public. Moreover, public discussion could bring together the empirical and conceptual strands that had previously existed as separate lines of inquiry in the written literature. A new discourse on the soviets began to develop that centered on practice rather than myth. At its heart were the related questions: What is really going on? What is to be done about it? Inasmuch as these questions concerned ostensibly public institutions, the soviets, answers to them would necessarily be formulated in terms of a public *in statu nascendi*. The discussion, in short, could move in only one direction—toward democracy.

As *perestroika* entered its second year, the professional literature on governmental institutions began to evince marked changes in the way in which it characterized Soviet political life. In the old discourse, 'bureaucracy' had been understood as an aberration, a negative phenomenon traceable to the personal shortcomings of officials, which expressed itself primarily as 'red tape'.[9] Now the concept was recast as a 'complex socio-economic phenomenon'[10] that had enabled an 'administrative elite' to usurp political power and use it to secure its own interests against those of the larger society.[11] The problems of political life, this literature emphasized, cannot be solved by following the longstanding prescriptions for further perfection of the administrative apparatus. Rather, the problem was this apparatus itself, the way that it was organized and its *de facto* monopoly of political power. Democracy was the only solution.[12]

This same candid language began to appear in public discussions of the soviets. Reversing the tenets of the old doctrine, the new discourse, with its emphasis on social practice, exposed the soviets as weak and ineffective institutions incapable of exerting any appreciable influence over the real holders of power, the party and state administrative hierarchies.[13] Citizens were now portrayed as understandably detached from public affairs, since they were well aware of the fact that the soviets lacked the power to represent their interests effectively and that they themselves were systematically denied information about, and access to, the real business of government.[14] Similarly, those elected to represent the public were now described as excluded from the decision-making process and given no meaningful information about it.[15]

Having dropped a few direct references of his own to the importance of democratic elections to the success of *perestroika*,[16] Gorbachev waded into this discussion himself at the January (1987) Plenum of the Central Committee of the CPSU. A measure of the moment occasioned by this gathering can be taken from the fact that it had been thrice postponed and had finally convened after the time limit between plena, as specified in the Party *Rules*, had already elapsed.[17] Gorbachev's opening address to the Plenum was remarkable on a number of accounts, two of which are of direct interest to us here. First, he reversed one of the main axes of conventional Soviet discourse by counterposing Leninism to political life in the USSR. This uncanny use of potent symbols by the General Secretary discredited at one stroke the entire ideational edifice of the political order. Rather than scientific theory and enlightened social practice (Leninism), he said, the USSR was ruled by 'dogma' and 'scholastic theorizing' which have 'exerted a negative influence on the solution of social questions.'[18]  Second, Gorbachev located the roots of the current malaise in the absence of democratic institutions and called for open, competitive elections in order to involve the population in the affairs of government and to weed out time-servers, retrogrades and incompetent officials.[19]

The Resolution adopted by the Plenum gave overall support to the democratic ideas voiced by Gorbachev, but in language much tamer than that employed by the General Secretary.[20]  A compromise had evidently been reached.  Rather than competitive elections across the board, an experiment was scheduled for June of that year in which some five per cent of deputies to district, town and village soviets would be elected in competitive races.[21]  More importantly, a Conference of the CPSU was to be called—the first one to be held since 1941—to deal with major questions of policy, prominent among which was now the issue of democratization.  As Gorbachev put it in his closing remarks to the January Plenum:

> That lever, comrades, that will enable us to provide *perestroika* with the decisive force is the people.  If we don't include the people, then we will neither solve the tasks of accelerating [our development], nor guarantee *perestroika* itself.  *Perestroika* simply will not be... We need democracy like we need air.[22]

Although the Plenum was unable to reach consensus on Gorbachev's radical proposals for democratization, it nonetheless produced the sort of compromise that would enable the proponents of political reform to carry their fight forward.  On one hand, the experimental elections to local soviets conducted in June of 1987 validated their view that, indeed, competitive elections were possible in the USSR.  What was a proposal, an argument, was now a fact.[23]  This fact was, of course, associated with the advance of *perestroika*, and the elections themselves could be dramatized as a significant public event by reform advocates and used to extend the struggle for reform.  Not only was the time right for the idea of competitive elections,[24] but the experience of these relatively open elections had flushed out *perestroika's* opponents whose anti-democratic machinations were now visible to all.  Accordingly, the press reported on how local officials manipulated nominations,[25] intimidated candidates in an effort to secure their withdrawal from certain races,[26] illegally substituted their own candidates for those apparently preferred by the voters,[27] and engaged in a substantial amount of ballot fraud to ensure the desired results.[28]  In the face of this, however, the will of the citizens at times won out[29] and some local political bosses were defeated, indicating that while the struggle ahead would be difficult, it was by no means hopeless.

On the other hand, the period leading up to the Nineteenth Party Conference, scheduled for June of 1988, witnessed an intensification of the attack on *perestroika's* opponents, now increasingly referred to by the sharper, more politically charged appellation, 'the apparatus'.  This reference, of course, was to the administrative apparatus of the Communist Party which, in the old discourse, had occupied the position of faithful servant toiling on behalf of the people.  In the discourse of democratization, however, the position of the apparatus was reversed. It now appeared as 'usurper' of the people's right to self-government,[30] as a power clique pursuing its own narrow interests,[31] as a bulwark of the old, discredited ways of Stalinism.[32]  Moreover, the circle of this discussion was expanded.  To the voices of journalists and specialists in the field of law and government were added, via published letters to the editor, the voices of people from all walks of life who identified the root of their problems as the closed world of officialdom that bred unwarranted privilege, self-aggrandizing power, reactionary attitudes and illegal practices.[33]

As this new, critical discourse on the want of democracy in the institutions of government gathered force, it began to depict in greater detail the real impotence of those same soviets that the old discourse had celebrated as 'authentic, authoritative institutions of people's power'.  Instead of 'tribunes' of the people, soviet deputies now appeared as individuals selected for office by the apparatus principally because of their docility.[34]  Whereas party members in the ranks of deputies had long enjoyed the mythic status of the 'guiding nucleus' of a given soviet, the politically advanced group of representatives who propounded and won support for the party's policies, the new discourse revealed that the work of a soviet's party group was but another ritual enacted on behalf of the apparatus, a ritual that effectively made a mockery not only of the soviet but of the party itself.[35]  In this respect, the new discourse severed what had been joined in the old.  The executive organs of soviets were split off from the full complement of deputies just as the party apparatus was counterposed to the party *per se*.  With these distinctions in place, a spectrum of power could be painted in which soviets appeared on the pale end as a mere 'façade'[36] behind which their executive organs easily, regularly and often illegally monopolized the entire business of government.[37] Yet these executive organs were themselves another façade, one that concealed the real power behind the scenes, that of the party apparatus.[38] By early 1988, a leading national newspaper published an interview with B. P. Kurashvili of the Soviet Academy of Sciences' Institute of State and Law in which he went so far as to resurrect Lenin's pre-revolutionary idea of 'dual power' in order to describe the present situation. Whereas in 1917 'dual power' represented the struggle between the old order (Russia's Provisional Government), and the Revolution (the soviets), today, said Kurashvili, it stood for the political leadership and the people, on one hand, and the apparatus on the other.[39] The new discourse of the reform movement could scarcely have drawn the lines of conflict in sharper relief.

The counterattack came as preparations were underway for delegate selection to the Nineteenth Party Conference. It appeared on 13 March in the form of a letter, purportedly written by a Leningrad schoolteacher and published in the daily, *Sovetskaya Rossiya*, which was laced with old-fashioned Stalinist rhetoric depicting *perestroika* as an enemy plot to undermine socialism and the nation as well.[40] The nature and context of this letter signalled an event of considerable magnitude. Its very appearance indicated that there was powerful support for the views it expressed among those in the higher circles. Right-wing elements in the apparatus seized on this opportunity to come out into the open to roll back the political changes under which they were already smarting.[41] In party organizations and factories throughout the country, meetings were hastily called 'to study' the letter and to propound what was being disseminated as a new (anti-*perestroika*) party line. Since the official media carried no reply from *perestroika* advocates for over three weeks, many were left to wonder at this time whether *perestroika* had not in fact been assassinated in an apparatus coup, leaving to the approaching Party Conference the task of writing out its death certificate.

On 5 April, however, *Pravda* finally broke the silence with an unsigned full-page editorial that delivered an official rebuke to the *Sovetskaya Rossiya* gambit. Other newspapers followed suit in even more strident terms, referring to Stalinism as the precursor of the Nazi occupation of the USSR which, emulating Stalin's policy of mass murder, sought to erase the nation by liquidating those most involved with the creation and transmission of its culture.[42] In the public discussion of governmental reform, the way was now open for yet sharper analyses of the reality and consequences of apparatus rule, for a full-scale assault on the opponents of democratization. A turning point had been reached. Either things would be called by their real names in public, or the sword of reaction would forever hang over the head of the reform. The only road open to democratization, it appeared, was the democratic one, one which included the citizenry in open discussion of the problems facing the country, one which involved them in working out *perestroika's* concrete course, a course which they could then be counted on to defend.

It would be an exaggeration to suppose that at this juncture some ideal of unconstrained political debate had been achieved in the USSR. It would be equally mistaken, however, not to note that the period immediately preceding the Nineteenth Party Conference represented an explosion of popular political activity unprecedented in the years of Communist Party rule. Mass demonstrations were staged in scores of cities throughout the country, condemning the repressive rule of the apparatus and, in particular, its nefarious role in rigging delegate selection to the upcoming Conference.[43] The newspaper, *Izvestiya,* ran reports on how the party apparatus—by now more or less synonymous in political discourse with 'anti-reform forces'—was hijacking the Party Conference by packing the complement of delegates (illegally and undemocratically) with hand-picked toadies.[44] It also opened its letters column to a cascade of criticism pouring in from readers around the country. Having no control over political and governmental affairs, wrote one, we play the role of the chorus in classical Greek drama. 'Little by little a situation has come about that Marx described as a government listening only to its own voice, knowing that it is listening only to its own voice, while it reinforces its own self-deception by requiring the people to sustain this self-deception by [echoing back] in their own voice the same [words].'[45] Now, another lamented, the Party Conference called to extend the process of democratization would be dominated by an 'apparatus of paid functionaries that has selected itself'.[46]

The opposition contained in the new discourse, that pitted the reform leadership and the people against a reactionary party apparatus, was coming to life before the eyes of the nation. On the eve of the Conference, Party Secretary G. P. Razumovskii spoke at a meeting in the

Kremlin convened to commemorate Lenin's birth. He used the occasion to associate the figure of Lenin with the reform movement and to discredit its opponents as anti-Leninist. Razumovskii told his audience that 'without democratization it is impossible to include the people in *perestroika* and what [then] remains are [only] abstract summonses to activate the human factor'. Underscoring the concrete and sweeping nature of the envisaged democratization, he added that 'the decisive voice in the selection and placement of cadres belongs to the masses'.[47] His words represented an authoritative pronouncement against the *nomenklatura* system of appointments in favour of a radically new principle of leadership selection, that of democratic elections. It remained for others to amplify this point.

The disease of bureaucracy has begun to reach a terminal stage in the USSR, wrote L. Ponomarev and V. Shinkarenko, as high officials develop ties with the criminal underworld. 'It can be said that this has given birth to our own home-grown mafia.'[48] Tatyana Zaslavskaya, sociologist and adviser to Gorbachev, linked the fate of *perestroika* to the struggle with the apparatus and its allies in the criminal underworld. Only by abolishing the *nomenklatura* system, she argued, could this struggle be won.[49] Others used the trope of 'the braking mechanism', a general term introduced years earlier by Gorbachev to label that which held back the progress of the country. 'The braking mechanism', wrote A. Demidov, 'is the *nomenklatura*'.[50] Others added that its mode of operation ensured the development and maintenance of an incestuous caste of officials, divorced from and opposed to the larger society.[51] It has promoted and protected incompetents, while it has bred conservatism and cynicism.[52] The *nomenklatura* has destroyed public life and public institutions.[53] It has come to represent, in short, the organized appropriation of public office for private gain on a grand scale.[54]

## CHARTING THE COURSE OF REFORM

In late May, the Central Committee of the CPSU convened to adopt a programme of reform that would serve as the framework for discussion at the Party Conference. The 'Theses' that emerged from this Plenum identified the party apparatus, in its ability to appropriate public office and abuse the public trust, as the principal opponent of reform and the chief reason for the country's slow progress during the first three years of *perestroika*.[55] In order to break the hold of the apparatus on the political life of society, the 'Theses' advocated what might be called a political *perestroika* on three broad fronts. First, competitive elections under secret ballot would replace the *nomenklatura* system of appointments as the means for selecting high-level party and soviet officials. Officeholders, in turn, would be limited to two five-year terms except in special cases in which a three-fourths majority could be obtained to extend their terms of office another five years.

Second, soviets would be restructured in order to free them from the tutelage of the party organs and the branch apparatuses of the centralized ministries, thus enabling them to act as authentic institutions of popular government. In this respect, the 'Theses' called for a separation of powers between the elected legislators and the executive departments of the soviets. These executive departments, the 'Theses' made clear, had not only been functioning outside the control of the soviets but had in fact served as the medium through which others—the party organs and branch apparatuses of the ministries—have been able to dominate the activities of the elected officials. The separation of powers would be effected by prohibiting (with rare exceptions) those in the executive departments of a given soviet from serving simultaneously as deputies to that same soviet. The legislative role of the deputies would be enhanced by the allotment of more paid leave from their places of employment to fulfil the demands of office, and by internally reorganizing soviets so that their executive departments would work under the supervision of prezidiums composed of elected deputies.

Finally, the 'Theses' called for the creation of a 'socialist government of laws' (*sotsialisticheskoe pravovoe gosudarstvo*), a concept that had been gaining currency in the professional literature on government and law.[56] It was defined by the 'Theses' as 'the supremacy and majesty of law, expressing the will of the people. State and party organs, social organizations, labour collectives, all officials and citizens must act on a strictly legal basis.' The 'Theses' pointed out that this principle would add an important feature to the concept of government that had prevailed in the USSR heretofore, since 'not only do the citizens bear responsibility before the state, but [now] the state also bears responsibility before the citizens'.[57]

With the exception of a few, not unimportant, additions that we meet in the next chapter, the basic outlines of political *perestroika* were thus fixed in the 'Theses' prepared for the Party Conference. The 'Theses' were broadly discussed in the press and the published results of public opinion surveys conducted before[58] and after[59] the May Plenum showed considerable popular support for their basic provisions. Interestingly, however, one proposal contained in the 'Theses' that subsequently evoked a storm of protest when it appeared in the draft of the Constitutional amendments proferred to society in October attracted little or no attention in the discussions leading up to the Party Conference. This proposal concerned the electoral mechanism and stated obliquely that certain 'alternatives' would be discussed at the Party Conference regarding the organization of the soviets, among them one involving 'the election of some of the deputies directly from the public organizations constituent in the political system of our society'. In its final version, this proposal specified that one-third of the deputies of all soviets would not be elected publicly but appointed by public organizations such as the Communist Party, the trade unions and various other official bodies under a procedure that awarded the decisive influence in most of these appointments to the apparatus of the party and its clients in other institutions. The *nomenklatura* would thus be perpetuating itself in part through the medium of the new electoral mechanism. We anticipate our discussion of the reform programme adopted at the Nineteenth Party Conference and the changes introduced later into the Constitution and Electoral Law of the USSR by noting two things about this provision in the 'Theses'.

First, democratic practice is still a novelty in the USSR. Athough the Soviet citizenry is 'learning democracy', in the words of the ubiquitous slogan, that learning is an ongoing and demanding process. The development of a political culture capable of giving life to and sustaining democratic institutions is no doubt underway in the USSR. Yet, by the same token, Soviet political culture today regularly evinces a number of shortcomings when matched up against the requisites of a thoroughgoing democratic order. We have occasion to comment on a number of these shortcomings below. Here, we note one, namely, the tendency to focus on big (and ill-defined) ideas such as 'democracy' and to neglect those details that specify what 'democracy' means in concrete terms. During the Constitutional assessment that took place in autumn of 1988, articulate spokesmen for democratization again and again expressed their shock and dismay at the idea of public organizations choosing deputies to soviets and argued that this provision ran contrary to the reform programme adopted at the Nineteenth Party

Conference. As we have seen, it in fact antedated the Conference by a month. At the time, however, no one seemed to notice.

Second, the provision for the selection of some complement of deputies by the public organizations was a conservative one. Like others that were added in the 'Resolutions' of the Nineteenth Party Conference (and yet others that appeared in the drafts of amendments to the Constitution and to the Electoral Law) its effect was to provide 'filters', to use the expression popular in the USSR, between the citizenry and the government. Some advocates of radical democratization in the USSR have looked with resignation on these filters, considering them as essential to political stability during a period in which deep changes are under way and when, accordingly, the potential for demagoguery and mass extremism is high. Yet all those with whom I have spoken agree on the answer to the question: Who stands to benefit from these filters? The apparatus.

This particular example is representative of a pattern that repeated itself throughout the time frame of this study. A rush of excitement, activity and hope for progress along the path to democracy would culminate in institutional changes containing democratic features but encumbered by a number of anti-democratic filters. Perhaps this is the outcome to be expected from a process of democratization initiated by the top leadership which must, after all, avoid alienating a number of important constituencies if it is to continue as the top leadership. At the same time, however, we should not miss the dynamic evinced by this process, a sort of dialectic of democratization, whereby popular enthusiasm, summoned by the Gorbachev leadership, would focus on the anti-democratic concessions that this leadership was simultaneously offering to the apparatus as assurance that its position in the political order would not be unduly jeopardized by democratization. These concessions, then, represented concrete issues around which democratic forces would organize and press their claims. They triggered a series of real battles that became the actual vehicles for popular involvement in the process of democratization. As we see in much of what follows, 'democratization from above' is not only an oxymoron but in certain respects a misnomer for democratization in the USSR. Although the Gorbachev leadership provided a space for democratic forces to organize and act, it could not command them to do so. Rather, it was those below, mobilized as much by a commonly perceived enemy—the apparatus, its usurpations, its tricks—as by a vision of a democratic future who came to represent the engine of democracy in the Soviet system.

## NOTES

1. This legislation was initiated by a 1957 decree of the Prezidium of the Supreme Soviet on improving the work of local soviets. Before it ran its course in 1986, the number of legal acts issued by soviets at various levels that ostensibly aimed at upgrading their role in the political system ran into the thousands, perhaps tens of thousands. The most important pieces of legislation in this corpus, according to Soviet officials and legal specialists, include: 'Law on the Basic Rights and Duties of Rural and Settlement Soviets' (1968); two decrees of the Prezidium of the Supreme Soviet in 1971, 'On the Basic Rights and Obligations of City and City District Soviets'; 'Law on the Status of Soviet Deputies' (1972); articles 146-147 of the Constitution of the USSR (1977); 'Law on the Basic Authority of Krai and Regional Soviets, Soviets of Autonomous Regions and Autonomous Okrugs' (1980); and Resolution of the Central Committee of the CPSU, the Prezidium of the Supreme Soviet of the USSR and the Council of Ministers of the USSR, 'On Measures to Enhance Further the Role and Increase the Responsibility of Soviets of People's Deputies for Accelerating Social and Economic Development in Light of the Decisions of the 27th Congress of the CPSU' (1986).
2. Ronald J. Hill, 'The Development of Local Government since Stalin's Death', Everett M. Jacobs (ed.), *Soviet Local Politics and Government* (London: George Allen and Unwin, 1983), pp. 18-33; Michael E. Urban, 'Local Soviets and Popular Needs: Where the Official Ideology Meets Everyday Life', Stephen White and Alex Pravda (eds.), *Ideology and Soviet Politics* (London: Macmillan, 1988), pp. 137-158.
3. Michael E. Urban and John McClure, 'The Folklore of State Socialism: Semiotics and the Study of the Soviet State', *Soviet Studies*, Vol. 35 (Oct., 1983), pp. 471-486; Michael E. Urban, 'The Structure of Signification in the General Secretary's Address', *Coexistence*, Vol. 25 (1987), pp. 187-210.
4. A. J. Greimas, *Structural Semantics* (Lincoln, NE: University of Nebraska Press, 1983).
5. Fredric Jameson, *The Prison-House of Language* (Princeton: Princeton University Press, 1972); *The Political Unconscious* (Ithaca, NY: Cornell University Press, 1981).
6. Among the best examples of this type of study are A.T. Leizerov, *Demokraticheskie formy deyatel'nosti mestnykh Sovetov* (Minsk: BGU, 1977); *Konstitutsionnyi printsip glasnosti raboty Sovetov narodnykh deputatov* (Minsk: BGU, 1981); V. A. Mal'tsev, 'Printsip podotchetnosti v sisteme mestnogo Soveta', (doctoral dissertation; Voronezh: Voronezh State University, 1979); and the survey conducted by a research team from the Institute of State and Law, 'Sovershenstvovat' koordinatsionnye funktsii Sovetov', *Sovetskoe gosudarstuo i pravo*, No. 1 (Jan., 1976), pp. 23-31
7. Ronald J. Hill, *Soviet Politics, Political Science and Reform* (Armonk, NY: M. E. Sharpe, 1980); Archie Brown, 'Political Science in the Soviet Union: A New Stage of Development?', *Soviet Studies*, Vol. 36 (July, 1984), pp. 317-344. For an outline of the development of Soviet society that depicts the

Gorbachev leadership as the more or less natural result of the emergence of a civil society, see Moshe Lewin, *The Gorbachev Phenomenon* (Berkeley: University of California Press, 1989).

8. For a discussion of the structural changes introduced into Soviet political discourse by Gorbachev, see Michael E. Urban, 'From Chernenko to Gorbachev: A Repoliticization of Official Soviet Discourse?', *Soviet Union*, Vol. 13, No. 2 (1986), pp. 131-161; 'Political Language and Political Change: Notes on the Gorbachev Leadership', P.J. Potichnyj (ed.), *The Soviet Union: Party and Society* (Cambridge: Cambridge University Press, 1988), pp. 87-106.

9. Michael E. Urban, *The Ideology of Administration: American and Soviet Cases* (Albany, NY: State University of New York Press, 1982), p. 107.

10. A. F. Zverev, 'V. I. Lenin o sushchnosti byurokratii i byurokratizma', *Sovetskoe gosudarstvo i pravo*, (Jan., 1987), pp. 44-51.

11. M. Piskotin, 'Strategiya upravleniya', *Sovety narodnykh deputatov*, (Dec., 1986), pp. 10-16; Yu A. Rozenbaum, 'Sistema raboty s kadrami v usloviyakh perestroiki', *Sovetskoe gosudarstvo i pravo*, No. 12 (Dec., 1986), pp. 11-20.

12. Piskotin, 'Strategiya...'; G. Barabashev, 'Glavnoe zveno samoupravleniya', *Sovety narodnykh deputatov*, (Jan., 1986), pp. 9-17; A. V. Obolonskii, 'Byurokraticheskaya deformatsiya soznaniya i bor'ba s byurokratizmom', *Sovetskoe gosudarstvo i pravo*, No. 1 (Jan., 1987), pp. 52-61; B. Markov, 'Byurokratizm—antipod demokratii', *Kommunist*, No. 11 (July, 1987), pp. 110-119.

13. E.g., A. Illarionov, 'Plan i oblplan', *Izvestiya* (30 Mar. 1986); G. Shipit'ko, 'Priroda ne proshchaet oshibok', *ibid.* (14 Aug. 1986); G. Ni-Li, 'Provintsial'naya istoriya', *ibid.* (11 Dec. 1986).

14. V. A. Kryazhkov, 'Glasnost' raboty Sovetov: sotsiologiya i pravo', *Sovetskoe gosudarstvo i pravo*, (Dec., 1986), pp. 35-42.

15. V. E. Odintsov, 'Bez melochnoi opeki', *Izvestiya* (18 Oct. 1986).

16. Stephen White has noted that Gorbachev was the only speaker at the 27th Congress of the CPSU, which met in February of 1986, to mention the idea of reforming the electoral system. See his 'Democratization in the USSR, (mimeo; Glasgow: Glasgow University, 1989), p. 4. However, the programme adopted at the Congress did contain an oblique reference to electoral reform by noting that 'the Party attaches great significance to perfecting the forms of people's representation, to developing the democratic principles of the Soviet electoral system'. See *The Programme of the Communist Party of the Soviet Union* (Moscow: Novosti, 1986) p. 50.

17. White, *loc. cit.*

18. 'O perestroike i kadrovoi politike partii: Doklad General'nogo secretarya Tsk KPSS M. S. Gorbacheva na Plenume Tsk KPSS 27 yanvarya 1987 goda', *Izvestiya* (28 Jan. 1987).

19. *Ibid.*

20. 'O perestroike: kadrovoi politike partii: Postanovlenie Plenuma Tsentral'nogo Komiteta Kommunisticheskoi partii Sovetskogo Soyuza', *Izvestiya* (29 Jan. 1987).

21. *Izvestiya* (29 Mar. 1987).

22. 'Zaklyuchitel'noe slovo General'nogo secretarya Tsk KPSS M. S. Gorbacheva na Plenume TsK KPSS 28 yanvarya 1987 goda', *Izvestiya* (30 Jan. 1987).

23. Another element of compromise evident in the experimental elections of 1987 was the fact that head-to-head competition between candidates for an office was eschewed in favour of 'multi-mandate' districts wherein a number of candidates, (usually about seven) would compete for a lesser number of seats (usually five). For an analysis of these elections, see Stephen White,

"Reforming the Electoral System', *The Journal of Communist Studies*, Vol. 4 (Dec., 1988), pp. 1-17; Jeffrey Hahn, 'An Experiment in Competition: The 1987 Elections to the Local Soviets', *Slavic Review*, Vol. 47 (Fall, 1988), pp. 434-447. For an authoritative account of the conception behind the experiment and the relevance of the experiment to reforms that would follow, see G. V. Barabashev, 'Izbiratel'nya kampaniya: tseli i sredstva', *Sovetskoe gosudarstvo i pravo*, No. 4 (April, 1987), pp. 3-12; 'Resurs neposredstvennoi demokratii', *Sovety narodnykh deputatov*, (July, 1987), pp. 17-24.

24.  For an example of this argument, see the Editorial, 'Demokraticheskii potentsial v deistvii', *Sovety narodnykh deputatov*, (Oct., 1987), pp. 3-6.

25.  V. Mirolevich, '29 izmerenii', *Izvestiya* (28 April 1987).

26.  Vladimir Nadein, 'Vybory v zerkale chuvstv', *Izvestiya* (18 July 1987).

27.  E. Andryushenko and V. Vasil'ev, 'Razmyshleniya posle vyborov', *Sovety narodnykh deputatov*, (Nov.,1987), pp. 92-98; esp., pp. 92-93.

28.  *Ibid.*, pp. 97-98; V. Shepotkin, 'Obnovlenie', *Izvestiya* (7 July 1987).

29.  E.g., Shepotkin, *loc. cit.*; M. Amaev, 'Golosovali protiv formalizma', *Izvestiya* (12 Apr. 1987); White, 'Reforming the Electoral System'.

30.  Boris El'tsin, then First Secretary of Moscow's City Committee of the CPSU, is quoted to this effect by V. Buldashov, 'Ot zamyslov—k delu', *Izvestiya* (17 Mar. 1987). See also Yu. Feofanov's interview with O. E. Kutafin, then Dean of the Law Faculty of Moscow State University, 'Deputat i apparat' *ibid.*, (13 Nov. 1987); and B. N. Topornin, 'Sovetskoe gosudarstvo i samoupravlenie naroda', *Kommunist*, No. 6 (Apr., 1987), pp. 80-89.

31.  Interestingly, two very similar essays on glasnost' and the operations of local government published by V. A. Kryazhkov are radically different in their analyses of the problems of scarce information for deputies and their consequent passivity. Prior to the January Plenum, Kryazhkov attributed the problem to state officials with a penchant for marking documents 'secret'. In an article published after the January plenum, however, he referred to restrictions on information as the results of 'intra-apparatus interests'. The articles in question are: 'Glasnost' raboty Sovetov: sotsiologiya i pravo', *Sovetskoe gosudarstvo i pravo*, No. 12 (Dec., 1986), pp. 35-42; and 'Uchit'sya glasnost'', *Sovety narodnykh deputatov*, (May, 1987), pp. 18-26.

32.  See the letters column in *Izvestiya* (9 Jan.1988).

33.  Michael E. Urban, 'Political Language in the Letters Column of a Soviet Newspaper', *Semiotext(e)* (forthcoming).

34.  See A. Speranskii's letter to the Editor, 'Pochemu ya ne znayu svoego deputata', *Izvestiya* (28 Dec. 1987).

35.  V. Boikov, 'Partgruppa: dela i plany', *Sovety narodnykh deputatov*, (Sept., 1987), pp. 82-85; Yu. Feofanov's interview with V. Chicheurov, *Izvestiya* (20 Mar. 1988).

36.  Nikolai Lisovenko and Yurii Feofanov, 'Troe v odnoi lodke', *Izvestiya* (23 Jan. 1988)

37.  N. Solnyak, 'Uroki odnoi sessii', *Sovety narodnykh deputatov*, (Jun., 1987), pp. 72-77; K. Lagunov, 'Naprasno nas sobrali', *Izvestiya* (14 July 1987).

38.  V. Vukovich, 'Inertsiya steriotipov', *Izvestiya* (4 Jan. 1988); 'Kak vybrali predsedatelya', *ibid.* (23 Mar. 1987); G. Shcherbina, 'V dva zakhoda', *ibid.* (1 Mar. 1988).

39.  Yu. Feofanov's interview with B. Kurashvili, *Izvestiya* (16 Feb. 1988).

40.  N. Andreeva, 'Ne mogu postupat'sya printsipami', *Sovetskaya Rossiya* (13 March 1988).

41.  Discussions of the Andreeva letter and its aftermath can be found in Eric F. Green, *The 19th Conference of the CPSU: Politics and Policy* (Washington, D.C.:

American Committee on US-Soviet Relations, 1988), pp. 5-7; Nikolai Shishlin, 'Perestroika and the Party', Robert J. Kinston (ed.), *Perestroika Papers* (Dubuque, Iowa: Kendall/Hunt, 1988), pp. 40-45; Dev Murarka, 'Gorbachev's Opposition: The Foes of *Perestroika* Sound Off', *The Nation*, Vol. 246 (21 May 1988), pp. 697, 714-718.

42. V. Dashichev, 'Vmesto dogmy—trud uma', *Izvestiya* (13 Apr. 1988).
43. Interview with Mikhail Malyutin of Moscow's Popular Front (30 Oct. 1988). On this topic, see my '"Informals" and Popular Fronts', *Detente*, No. 14 (1989), pp. 3-8, 27; Boris Kagarlitsky, 'The Truth About *Perestroika*', *The Nation*, Vol. 248 (5 June 1989), pp. 765-767.
44. Vladimir Nadein, 'Vtoroi dolzhen byt' zhenshchina?', *Izvestiya* (14 May 1988).
45. Quoted by Yurii Orlik, 'Pravo vybora', *Izvestiya* (23 Apr. 1988).
46. Quoted by Yurii Orlik, 'Uroki na zavtra', *Izvestiya* (11 June 1988).
47. G. P. Razumovskii, 'Za obnovlenie sotsializma, za leninizm', *Izvestiya* (23 Apr. 1988).
48. L. Ponomarev and V. Shinkarenko, 'Chem silen byurokrat?', *Izvestiya* (18 May 1988).
49. See her interview with E. Manucharova, 'Korennoi vopros perestroiki', *Izvestiya* (4 Jun. 1988).
50. Letter to the Editor, *Izvestiya* (30 May 1988). See also F. Petrenko's letter published in *Kommunist*, No. 9 (Jun., 1988), pp. 36-38.
51. See the letters excerpted by Yurii Orlik, 'S mysl'yu o konferentsii', *Izvestiya* (16 Apr. 1988); Yurii Burtin, 'Svoboda vybora', *ibid.* (29 Apr. 1988); B. Kharchenko, 'Cherez golovy Sovetov', *Pravda* (13 May 1988); G. Ni-Li, 'Sovsem ne lichnye schety', *Izvestiya* (5 Jun. 1988).
52. See the survey data presented by Ponomarev and Shinkarenko, 'Chem silen byurokrat?'; and V. Orlov's interview with A. V. Sudakov, *Pravda* (26 May 1988).
53. A revealing statement to this effect can be found in the letter of a soviet official, R. Makarenko, that was published in *Literaturnaya gazeta*, No. 24 (15 Jun. 1988), p.11. The President of the Belorussian Supreme Soviet, G. S. Tarazevich, went so far as to account for the unique case of a local soviet actually functioning properly by noting that in the new town where the soviet was organized no party committee had yet been formed. See his 'Avtoritet i vlasti', *Izvestiya* (23 Jun. 1988).
54. See Demidov's letter, *supra*. See also the letter by A. Kuibyshev, *Izvestiya* (13 Jun. 1988).
55. 'Tezisy Tsentral'nogo Komiteta KPSS k XIX Vsesoyuznoi partiinoi konferentsii', *Izvestiya* (23 May 1988).
56. A clear statement of this idea can be found in V. O. Mushinskii, 'Sootnoshenie politiki i prava v regulirovanii sotsial'nykh interesov', *Sovetskoe gosudarstvo i pravo*, No. 2 (Feb., 1988), pp. 3-12.
57. The 'Theses' went on to note the implications of a 'government of laws' for the Soviet court system and how it would have to be improved and protected from political interference. It stopped short of drawing the obvious conclusion, however, that a 'government of laws' can only be secured on the basis of an independent judiciary. For a lucid presentation of the connection of law and the independence of the court system in the Soviet context, see Yu. Feofanov, 'Vlast' i pravo', *Izvestiya* (21 Jun. 1988).
58. V. Shastakovskii and V. Yatskov, 'Demokratizatsiya partii—democratizatsiya obshchestva', *Kommunist*, No. 9 (Jun., 1988), pp. 31-35.

59.  See the results of a survey conducted by the Centre for the Study of Public
     Opinion of the Institute of Sociology in the Academy of Sciences of the
     USSR that appeared in *Izvestiya* (27 Jun. 1988).

# 3. THE PROJECT AND THE PROCESS

The Nineteenth Party Conference represented a decisive turning point in the process of democratization. On the one hand, it provided an occasion for an unprecedented outpouring of popular political activity in the form of mass meetings and street demonstrations that were staged by independent groups in scores of Soviet cities. The call for democracy, issued 'from above', was receiving an enthusiastic response 'from below'. On the other hand, the proceedings of the Conference, which were carried to a mass audience via Soviet television, made for another equally unprecedented event. Day after day, Soviet viewers were able to watch real political debates erupt on their television sets, debates that featured not only sharp disagreements within the Communist Party, but also a number of attacks on the ruling apparatus and certain of its members with Politburo rank. Speakers argued that this apparatus had grown fat on its privileges, out of touch with the population and oblivious to the requirements of the present day. It was culpable, they claimed, for economic mismanagement on a grand scale and directly responsible for the innumerable problems and incalculable social costs that this mismanagement produced. Many in the apparatus, including some at the top, were charged with abetting, or themselves engaging in, systematic corruption.

To read this event, however, as simply a clash between the forces of conservatism and those representing the project of democratic reform would be to miss its deeper significance. The Nineteenth Conference was the opening phase of a process that transformed the political order of the Soviet Union. As such, it initiated the transition from democratization as a general desideratum to *this particular democratization*, a specific set of institutions and practices to be realized here and now. The movement from the general to the specific, in turn, brought to the fore the double-sided contradiction inherent in democratization from above.

One side of this contradiction concerned the fact that the Gorbachev leadership depended on some degree of consensus within the hierarchy of power in order to produce a programme of political reform. Yet democratization implied that this very hierarchy would surrender some of its power to society. As long as democratization had been a general and ambiguous goal, disagreements within the hierarchy could be contained relatively easily. Even those who had nothing but distaste for the idea could publicly pay lip-service to it, while furtively working to block any measures that might disrupt the *status quo*. However, with concrete proposals on the table, the situation was radically altered. Now the question became *this* set of measures and its implications for *this* or *that* official in the hierarchy. Whose power was to be surrendered and how much of it? In order to contain the divisions introduced by such questions, some form of mediation was required. This took the form of bargaining. As in the instance of Gorbachev's radical democratic proposals to the January Plenum of the Central Committee in 1987, compromise again lined the road to consensus around a joint programme. At the Nineteenth Conference and during its aftermath, intra-elite differences were papered over by a sort of insurance policy that the elite took out on its common programme. The insurance was, of course, the anti-democratic 'filters' that were inserted at strategic points into the electoral process. Like fuses in an electrical system, these would guarantee that the democratic current could be switched off when its voltage was running uncomfortably high for certain elements in the elite.

The second aspect of the contradiction attending the process of democratization from above involved the authorities and the public. Obviously, the success of a programme for democratization that has been prepared by the authorities would, in the end, depend on the response of the citizens. Would they regard the programme as authentic and embrace it as their own? Would they breathe life into the project by participating in the new institutions that the authorities had created? In order to bridge the divide separating the authorities from the public, another mediation was required. It also had two sides, one visible and the other concealed. The visible side took the form of legislative activity, with provision for ostensible comment from the public, that would redesign the institutions of the Soviet state in order to make it possible for the citizenry to elect its leaders in a democratic way. The hidden side involved the spinning of a new myth about this legislative activity and the role of the public in it. Paradoxically, the legislative activity was, in fact, of symbolic rather than instrumental import, while the myth-making, although rich in affect and symbolism, represented the instrumental element that brought about change in the practical order. We can untangle these paradoxes by referring to the conventional accounts of the Constitutional reform and legislative changes that occurred in 1988 and locating the element of myth within them.

## SHADOW AND SUBSTANCE

In the conventional version of these events, the Nineteenth Conference of the CPSU adopted a series of resolutions on political reform that called for the introduction of competitive elections, the establishment of the rule of law and a restructuring of the USSR's governmental institutions. These resolutions served as a compass that guided the efforts of a 'working group' of legal specialists who assisted a Joint Commission of the Supreme Soviet on Legislative Proposals in producing draft amendments to the Constitution of the USSR and a draft of a new Electoral Law.[1] Following a period of about one month, during which these drafts were debated by the public in meetings, in the press and through the electronic media, and on the basis of criticisms and suggestions generated by this public discussion[2], the Commission on Legislative Proposals submitted revised drafts of the Constitutional amendments and Electoral Law to an extraordinary session of the Supreme Soviet which, after due deliberation, adopted the proposals as law.[3] This process, itself an example of the new, democratic orientation in politics that emerged at the Nineteenth Conference, opened the door to competitive elections in the USSR and ushered in a new era of Soviet democracy.[4]

As we shall see, there is very little in the above version of events that approaches the status of fact and a great deal in it that is pure fiction. For the moment, we might note a few features of this conventional characterization of the reform which indicate that it is myth and symbol, rather than instrumental legislative action, with which we are dealing. First, the preparatory subcommission of the Supreme Soviet's Joint Commission on Legislative Proposals represented the only group of would-be legislators who actually worked on the reform project. This subcommission, however, was not formed until 25 October; that is, a few days after the draft amendments and draft law had been promulgated.[5] Second, the period for public discussion was very short. Given delays in the postal system, a great number of letters to newspapers or to the authorities on the proposed changes did not reach their destinations until after the final drafts had been prepared. Moreover, as we see below, the 'regularized irregularities' of process for which Soviet politics is renown played a major role in the deliberations, one that seems to have distorted considerably the image of public commentary that was conveyed through the mass media back to the public itself. Finally, the Constitutional amendments and new Law on Elections cannot be regarded as institutional changes that made possible the competitive elections that followed their adoption. There is nothing in either the unamended Constitution or the old Electoral Law to prevent competitive elections. Nor is there anything in either the Constitutional amendments or the new Electoral Law to require them. Moreover, as we have seen, competitive elections had already been held on an experimental basis in 1987. They occurred again in by-elections to republic-level soviets in the autumn of 1988, prior to the publication of the new draft amendments and Electoral Law.[6]

The Constitutional and legislative changes, then, cannot be regarded as instrumental activity in the sense that they altered the legal system of the USSR in order to enable democratization to go forward. Rather, they promoted the process of democratization in an altogether different way, a way that was *politically* instrumental. On the one hand, intra-elite differences were contained by means of compromises that, as we shall see, diluted the formal democratic aspects of the legal structures. Ironically, if the Soviet system was to become more democratic in practice, the price exacted by the compromises with conservatives meant that it would be less democratic in principle. On the other hand, the project itself, along with the nationwide assessment that followed its promulgation, served to publicize the fact that the political system was indeed undergoing democratic changes and that the citizenry were invited to involve themselves in it. Politically active individuals responded to this invitation but, with no less irony, they most often did so by registering their opposition to the proposed legislation changes, especially to the 'filters' that had been implanted in the electoral procedures and governmental machinery in order to appease conservatives in the apparatus.

We therefore arrive at the view that the project and process of legislative reform resembled a massive rite of passage that prepared Soviet society for a transition from one political order to another by integrating around a common endeavour what would otherwise have been opposing forces speaking in either discordant voices or stony silence. The project and its assessment provided all with the opportunity to engage in a common argument. With respect to the legislative changes that were ultimately introduced, however, the content of this argument was perhaps less important than the simple fact that it took place.

## POLITICAL DIVISIONS

As the idea of democratization began to assume a concrete form in the Resolutions of the Nineteenth Party Conference and, more so, in the drafts of the Constitutional amendments and Electoral Law that appeared in the autumn of 1988, the parties to this argument began to divide themselves into three broad groupings. On the right stood the conservative apparatus; on the left, those who were committed to a vision of democratization that went considerably beyond what the authorities were prepared to offer; and, in the centre, the authorities themselves who, under Gorbachev's leadership, managed the entire affair, in large part by reaching accommodation with the right-wing. In this respect, the project altered the constellation of political forces in Soviet society. Prior to the Nineteenth Conference, the main lines of conflict were drawn, as we have seen, between those advocating democratization and those in the apparatus who felt their power and privileges threatened by it. However, once a specific project had been formulated, one fashioned out of a series of centre-right compromises, a split occurred within the democratic camp, dividing those who formerly had spoken in similar voice about the desideratum of democratization into one group (the centre) who would defend the project, and another (the left) who would attack it. Inasmuch as we have occasion to consider in some detail the views expressed by these two groups in what follows, we might at this point say a word about those who played a

minor role in the debates on the project but a major role, behind the
scenes, in framing it; namely, the apparatus.

In the same way that the apparatus was able to manipulate the
selection of delegates and secure for itself a commanding majority at
the Nineteenth Conference[7]—with the ironic result that the Conference,
called in part for the purpose of extending democracy, became primarily
an occasion to complain about alleged excesses of democracy that had
already taken place[8]—it no doubt regarded the reforms initiated there
as changes in procedure that it could easily master and control by
methods in which it was well practised. The 'leadership' or 'assistance'
provided to soviets by the apparatus had always been an euphemism for
the fact that party organs had stage-managed every phase of soviet
work, from naming the deputies to scripting their agendas, to writing
the decisions that soviets would issue in their own name.[9] Is it likely
that the apparatus would fear competitive elections *per se* as a threat to
its control over the process by which the selection of deputies would
take place? Judging from published accounts of the party's role in the
competitive experimental elections of 1987 and the by-elections of
1988, the answer would be 'perhaps not'. Each instance demonstrated
that the party organs were relatively successful in warding off challenges to their hold on the reins of power. They continued to control the
majority of outcomes under conditions of electoral competition because
they were able to deploy their power in the nominations process, as they
had always done, to prevent those whom they did not endorse from
getting on the ballot. As the Soviet journalist, Yu. V. Feofanov, put it
during an interview:

> First of all, no one wants to give up power. Secondly, you know, there
> is a purely pragmatic thing here. That is, the party apparatus doesn't know
> any other way to act than what they've got used to doing. When other
> candidates [in addition to those selected by the apparatus] were put
> forward, the party organs, and not just the *raikom* but the factory party
> committees, smeared them.[10]

A look at the world of politics refracted through the medium of internal
party documents offers some compelling reasons as to why the apparatus would seem to have little to fear from electoral competition.

The Sovetskii District in the Moscow Region was one of the sites
chosen for the electoral experiment of 1987. Under the rules of the
experiment, individual single-member electoral districts were com-

bined into larger 'multi-mandate' constituencies in which a plurality of candidates would stand for election to a specified number of seats. In order to be elected to one of the seats in a given constituency, a candidate had to receive a majority of votes and also place among the top vote-getters, with 'top' defined as the number equal to the number of seats in that constituency. Candidates who received a majority of votes but were not among the top vote-getters would become 'reserve deputies' (entitled to participate as non-voting members of the soviet and to replace deputies who might leave office before the expiration of their terms), while those who failed to obtain a majority vote would simply be defeated.

One of the internal party documents under consideration explains how the local party apparatus, the *raikom*, drew up the boundaries for the multi-mandate constituencies in the Sovetskii District, determined the number of seats (between three and five) that would be contested in each, and designated the number of candidates ('as a rule, one [extra] candidate') who would stand for election in each constituency.[11] The document went on to outline how candidates were selected, noting that officials from the *raikom* would visit their counterparts in the party, trade union and Komsomol organizations of local enterprises which had the right to nominate candidates in order to collect a list of names in each that was preferred by those working at the bottom levels of these apparatuses. Those on the lists were then vetted by means of informal conversations with employees in the respective enterprises. The names selected by the *raikom* officials were thereafter proposed to meetings of the labour collectives in those enterprises nominating candidates. These meetings, the document made clear, were orchestrated by officials from the *raikom*. In some instances, the number of candidates nominated in this way exceeded the limit that had been established earlier by the apparatus. Consequently, the electoral commissions, on instructions from the *raikom*, declined to register a number of those who had been nominated.

A second document, prepared by the *raikom*'s propaganda department, recounted how the apparatus, following instructions from the Moscow *obkom*, conducted the election campaign.[12] The propaganda department organized a number of meetings in each district where the candidates could speak to the voters and answer their questions. Turnout was ensured by holding the management of enterprises responsible for the attendance of their workers. In a reversal of, say, the American pattern in which candidates for office recruit their respective campaign staffs, this document discussed how a staff at-the-ready, the local party apparatus and activists, went about recruiting candidates, schooled them to perform the roles for which they had been chosen, and then staged their campaigns. The only problems that the apparatus seemed to have encountered in conducting electoral campaigns under the new conditions of electoral competition were: (a) the enlarged electoral districts, with a number of candidates in each, required more voters' meetings to be held than had previously been the case, leading some voters to complain that 'we are already tired of all these meetings'; and (b) the propaganda department, with more information to collect and publish on more candidates, ended up running out of paper.

Finally, a third document, prepared jointly by the First Secretary of the Sovetskii *raikom*, the Director of the House of Political Enlightenment in the Moscow *obkom*, and an instructor from the Executive Committee of the Moscow Regional Soviet, provides some insight into how the authorities assessed their encounter with electoral competition.[13] The document recounts how the apparatus organized the polling on election day, lists the number of voters whom the apparatus managed to turn out, and describes how non-voters were subsequently called to account for their absence from the polls by officials of the *raikom* in the presence of their workplace supervisors. Some 'accidents' are also noted. These involve officials of the district soviet who either failed to win back their seats on the soviet and were relegated to the status of reserve deputies, or who managed to retain their seats only by a narrow margin. These 'accidents' were attributed to certain 'problems' in the new arrangement for electoral competition, problems that the experiment brought to the fore. In the words of the document:

> Not all the population is ready to participate in the experimental form of elections, since personal interests and a consumer orientation directly influence the voting, such that some of the voting results have literally cast the most principled workers of the soviets into the status of reserve deputies.

On the basis of what these documents contain, it would seem that local elites could adjust their methods of rule to conditions of electoral competition. They controlled the electoral process from start to finish and, except for a few 'accidents', were able to determine the corpus of deputies elected to the soviets. Moreover, a mass survey with some

25,000 respondents conducted in early 1988 by the Academy of Social Sciences under the Central Committee of the CPSU, provided additional reasons to suggest that the ruling apparatus had little to fear from democratic competition for office. The majority of respondents did not endorse the principle of competitive elections[14] and only 7.7 per cent of them felt that restructuring was needed in the area of soviet work.[15] As two of the researchers put it, 'if this continues further, then the bureaucrats will be able to sleep peacefully.'[16] As we have noted, the apparatus was already under challenge from a section of the Soviet intelligentsia that was committed to democratization. But this group did not seem to be large in number, had no apparent mass audience and, judging from the outcome of one of its attempts to ignite controversy on the fate of *perestroika* at the Nineteenth Party Conference[17], could easily be pushed into the background.

## FORMULATION OF THE PROJECT: STAGE I

Although the Nineteenth Party Conference placed the matter of competitive elections on the top of the USSR's political agenda, throughout four days of debate in which scores of speakers took part, remarkably little was said about introducing competitive elections. Gorbachev raised the matter in his opening remarks before the Conference, and spoke of 'the need for a resolute renewal of our election system ... that would ensure the right to nominate an unlimited number of candidates ... enabling the voters to elect ... militant, politically competent and vigorous people ... as effectively as possible.'[18] In his speech to the Conference two days later, Gorbachev mentioned his experience as a city and regional party secretary and how he had observed at first-hand the way in which the party apparatus dominated the work of the soviets. In order to correct this situation, he continued, democratic elections to the soviets would be required.[19] However, only two other speakers commented on the question of elections. One endorsed opening up the nominations process at the local level;[20] another, quoting Lenin, insisted that an end to the party's ability to control the placement of personnel would mean an end to the party's ability to set and implement policy.[21]

As if to strike a balance between such opposing views regarding the party's proper relationship with the soviets, Gorbachev surprised his audience at the Nineteenth Conference with a major proposal that had not been included in the Central Committee's 'Theses' that were meant to serve as the substantive framework for discussion. After endorsing a notion highlighted in the 'Theses' that there must be strict demarcation between the functions of the party and state bodies, he appeared to reverse himself by contending that 'the most practical way [to enhance the role of elected bodies] would be to nominate, as a rule, first secretaries of party committees to serve as chairmen of the respective soviets.'[22] Rather than curtailing the unwarranted intrusion of party bodies in the affairs of soviets, this measure struck many as a way to institutionalize it.

This proposal became the focus of effectively all the discussions that took place at the Conference with respect to reforms in the political system.[23] The other features of the political reform that had been outlined in the 'Theses' of the Central Committee and expanded in the 'Resolutions' that the Conference unanimously adopted, scarcely provoked a word from the delegates. Indeed, until the drafts of the new Law on Elections and amendments to the Constitution appeared in October, public discussion of political reform seemed riveted to the issue of whether the combination of the offices of first secretary of a party committee and chairmanship of the corresponding soviet would advance or hinder the cause of political *perestroika*.[24] The proposal's capacity to deflect attention from the larger blueprint of political reform was the first of its remarkable qualities.

The second was its devilish logic. Repeating the arguments of B. P. Kurashvili, who appeared to have been the initial source of the proposal,[25] Gorbachev noted two direct benefits that would follow from the combination of these offices. On the one hand, 'if the first secretary of a party committee [were] elected chairman of the respective soviet, this [would] raise the soviet's prestige ...'[26] The power and authority of the party apparatus would thereby be harnessed to the task of empowering soviets, converting them into real *loci* of decision and action. On the other hand, this combination of offices would have the potential to alter power relations within the apparatus itself by making its leading figures 'more effectively answerable to the working people because the elections at the sessions [of soviets] will be conducted by secret ballot. This means that the mandate received by a party leader from Communists will be verified and confirmed by representatives of the people ...'[27] From this perspective, political power would be asked to step forward and show its face. Party leaders would, as chairpersons of soviets, now be held publicly accountable for the decisions that they as party leaders had been making all along. Moreover, since the deputies of their respective soviets would have the legal right to confirm them as chairpersons, their power would now rest in constituencies far broader than the narrow circles of the *nomenklatura*. And should the deputies vote down the nominations of these party leaders, perhaps their party organizations would 'draw the necessary conclusions'[28] and replace them.

This proposal was among the many resolutions endorsed by the Conference on its final day of work. Others which, taken together, completed the initial stage of drafting the reform project included:

(1) The creation of a USSR Congress of People's Deputies which would function as 'the country's supreme body of authority' comprising, in addition to the deputies representing territorial and national-territorial constituencies, others representing the principal elements of the political system—the party, the trade unions, the Komsomol, other mass public organizations, as well as cooperative, creative and scientific associations—all of whom should be democratically elected at congresses or plenary meetings of their governing bodies.[29] The Congress would meet annually to decide the country's most important constitutional, political and socio-economic issues and would elect a 'relatively small bicameral USSR Supreme Soviet—a standing legislative, administrative and supervisory body—and elect by secret ballot the President of the Supreme Soviet.'[30]

(2) Electoral competition with 'unlimited nomination of candidacies' would be the method for selecting deputies to soviets at all levels. Elected officials would be limited to two consecutive five-year terms of office.[31]

(3) Each soviet would elect the leaders of its executive committee on the basis of multiple nominations and secret ballot. Members of the executive committee (with the single exception of its chairperson) would not be eligible to serve as deputies in their respective soviets. Deputies, in turn, would be relieved of some portion of their work obligations in order to devote more time to their responsibilities as legislators and monitors of the operations of the executive departments of government.[32]

(4) Leadership of the soviets would now be exercised by newly-created prezidiums, formed in all soviets above the level of the rural

village or urban settlement, that would be composed entirely of elected deputies.

(5) A 'socialist rule-of-law state' (*sotsialisticheskoe pravovoe gosudarstvo*) must anchor social, political and economic relations in the USSR.[33] 'Accordingly, to make law and government decisions conform strictly to the requirements of the Constitution of the USSR, it would be useful to set up a Committee of Constitutional Oversight.'[34] In order to remove local political influences from the dispensing of justice, 'the unconditional independence of judges [will be secured by] the election of district, city, area, regional and territorial courts by superior soviets of people's deputies.'[35]

Although these provisions formed the kernel of the 'drafts of legislative acts on the restructuring of government bodies' that the Conference commissioned,[36] this phase of formulating a definite project for democratization left a great many matters unresolved. Who would have the right to nominate candidates for office? What powers would belong to the envisaged Congress of People's Deputies? Who would serve on the 'relatively small' Supreme Soviet and what would its relation be to the Congress? How would the Committee for Constitutional Oversight be composed and what authority would it have? These and a myriad of related questions were taken up by the 'working groups' who hammered out the details of the project as it entered its second phase.

## FORMULATION OF THE PROJECT: STAGE II

Very little has yet been made public with respect to how and by whom the drafts of the Constitutional amendments and Electoral Law were composed. Interest in the question of authorship, however, has been expressed both in the press and at public meetings. 'It is a pity,' said one legal specialist in reference to the anonymity of the drafters, 'the country needs to know its heroes'.[37] In the words of another, 'I know who wrote the American Constitution, and who wrote the French Constitution, but not who wrote my own.'[38]

The authoritative accounts that have appeared on the questions of how the drafts were produced and by whose hand have been rather short on specifics. According to V. Vasil'ev, a member of one of the working groups that drafted the Constitutional amendments, two groups were formed in August of 1988 by the Prezidium of the Supreme Soviet, one to prepare a new Law on Elections, the other to compose a series of amendments to the Constitution. Each working group was made up of legal specialists from the academic world and a number of 'responsible workers' from the Prezidium and the Central Committee of the CPSU. Vasil'ev went on to note obliquely that many disputes arose in the working groups but that these were argued out within a 'common language'.[39]

In conversations with some of the members of these working groups, I was informed that each was made up of about fourteen members, all of whom participated as equals in group discussions. Candidate member of the Politburo, Gorbachev confidant and future Vice-President of the USSR, A. I. Luk'yanov, exercised general direction over the groups and participated in most of their working sessions. Attendance at these sessions was rather fluid, due both to chronic absences on the part of some members, who in certain cases did not attend meetings and in others were not notified that meetings were scheduled, and to occasional visits from other high-ranking officials.

The procedures followed by the working groups were not entirely clear to the members themselves. Each group drafted various preliminary proposals, sometimes in variants, that were then sent to other working groups that had been organized in the apparatus of the Central Committee of the CPSU. The existence of these latter groups has not, to my knowledge, been mentioned in the press. Nor did those working under the Prezidium of the Supreme Soviet with whom I spoke (four legal specialists from institutions of higher education and a 'responsible worker' from the Prezidium's apparatus) appear to know much about the membership of these Central Committee groups. Proposals composed initially by the Prezidium's working groups passed through the hands of their counterparts in the Central Committee who often made changes in them before relaying them on to a circle of advisers that reported directly to Gorbachev. In some instances, disputed points were submitted to the Politburo for final decision, usually in the form of draft options from which the political leadership would chose.[40] On other occasions, however, the working groups received specific instructions from 'Gorbachev's circle' on issues which they had not themselves addressed. In these cases, the job of the working groups was reduced to translating the instructions into the vernacular of the Soviet legal profession, sometimes in the face of their own opposition to the measures themselves.[41]

Operating within the imprecise guidelines supplied by the Nineteenth Party Conference and the more specific directives and constraints issuing from their opposite numbers in the Central Committee apparatus and Gorbachev's circle, the Prezidium's working groups addressed themselves to two broad questions. First, how might the institutions of popular government be redesigned in order for soviets to act as authentic legislatures? Second, what role should democratic elections play in determining the composition of these newly-empowered legislative bodies? The members of the working groups with whom I spoke understood these questions to be mutually related, yet opinions varied on the precise nature of the interrelationship. Those subsequently described as holding the 'minority' view envisaged effective legislatures and democratic elections as a seamless whole. As one commented during an interview:

> Now, unfortunately, many of our democratic institutions don't work, in particular the system of soviets. Either they don't discharge their representative functions or they do so in a purely formal way ... The basic evil that we're trying to correct, the basic lack that we're trying to fill, involves promoting the democratization of the representative institutions.[42]

Others in the 'majority', however, tended to downplay the element of democracy and to express reservations about whether the Soviet population was prepared to shoulder the burden of choosing its government in a responsible way. As one put it afterwards during a public debate on the draft amendments to the Constitution, 'we got this Constitution because of who we are, our own customs and our own unreadiness for democracy'.[43]

The minimalist position regarding democratic elections was represented in the final documents issued by the working groups and defended thereafter by all members who offered public comment on the legislative projects that they had drafted regardless of their own personal views on the various provisions contained therein. Although a majority on both of the Prezidium's working groups might have adopted a minimalist position on the question of democracy in general, a majority could not be found for certain anti-democratic provisions that were simply stipulated to the working groups by their opposite numbers in the Central Committee or by Gorbachev's circle. In at least two instances, the working groups wrote into the drafts new electoral procedures—one involving pre-electoral district meetings, the other, specific provisions governing the selection of one-third of the deputies to all soviets by public organizations—that few if any of their members supported. This feature of the process was symptomatic of the overall compromise with power reached by the legal specialists on the working groups. Many of these individuals were among those discussed in the previous chapter who had laboured for a more democratic polity during the long, lean years of Brezhnev and the ensuing interregnum. Now, under Gorbachev, they were invited to bring their ideas into the world of practical politics but, in so doing, were required to sheer them of those elements that power found distasteful. Ironically, they wound up writing and defending not a few proposals that many or most of them did not themselves endorse. The process of drafting the Constitutional amendments and Electoral Law, then, took place within the context of a grand compromise with power, one that focused on empowering legislative bodies at all levels in the government and on reducing the formal democratic features of the electoral system that were already in place. In sum, the grand compromise involved replacing the existing system of sham legislatures whose members had been chosen by means of equal voting in direct (but non-competitive) elections with real legislatures that were to be selected by means of unequal voting in indirect elections in which some measure of competition would be possible.

What model should be used in designing these new legislatures? A new debate was already underway within the community of legal specialists regarding the form of representative institutions best suited to Soviet society. At one pole were those who favoured reviving Lenin's conception of 'the commune state' in which soviets appear as 'working corporations'.[44] Proponents of this view were, of course, well aware of the fact that this image of soviets had been hypocritically celebrated for decades by the very regime that had eviscerated soviets as organs of government. Their aim, however, was to realize in practice what had been paid lip service for so long.

According to their view, the state structure proper to a socialist society is one in which the distance between state and society is continually diminished. Through the system of soviets, citizens directly attend to their common affairs. They do so by electing a great number of their fellows to serve as deputies on soviets, and by participating themselves in a variety of administrative and quasi-administrative

bodies that are attached to soviets. Deputies do not form a special group
like legislators in Western democracies. They are amateurs, not profes-
sionals, who convene infrequently to reach decisions on public matters,
while retaining their regular full-time jobs and thus their direct contacts
with those whom they represent. Equally, the idea of 'checks and
balances' among the institutions of government is replaced by a fusion
of legislative, executive and judicial power. Government should be as
proximate as the deputy who works beside you on the factory floor, and
as simple and transparent as the session of the soviet whose members
reach a given decision and then, along with their fellow citizens, see to
its implementation in their places of employment and residence.[45]
From this perspective, the course charted by Lenin, in which the
institutions of the soviets represent a higher form of democracy con-
sonant with the very nature of a socialist society, should be the one
followed today.[46]

In opposition to this view, a number of those legal specialists concerned with the matter of political reform have come out in favour of
some version of parliamentary government for the USSR. Inasmuch as
Lenin's soviets have always been portrayed as an advance over parlia-
ments (in the same way that a socialist economy has represented an
advance over capitalism), advocates of this approach have had to defend
their readiness to take an apparent step backward. 'Yes, backward,' one
of them mentioned in a discussion of this point, 'backward to what we
never had!' As another proponent of parliamentary government
summed up the argument:

> We have tried for 70 years to realize the vision of the Marxist commune
> state. And these 70 years have shown that it doesn't work. The concept
> itself is mistaken. We need to adopt what does work, parliamen-
> tarianism.[47]

B. P Kurashvili and Fedor Burlatskii have been the most visible
proponents of parliamentary government in the USSR.[48] Neither
served on the Prezidium's working groups, but their ideas were well
known to a number of legal specialists who did.[49] Since the versions
of parliamentary government propounded by Kurashvili and Burlatskii
at the time were rather truncated, certain elements associated with their
proposals could be included into the reform project without at the same
time introducing either a full-blown parliamentary system in the Soviet
Union, or the more limited version of 'Soviet parliamentarianism' that

they espoused. Kurashvili, however, anticipated that the political reforms about to be fashioned by the working groups would fail to satisfy his minimal parliamentary criteria[50] and complained later that, indeed, this was unfortunately true.[51]

Members of the Prezidium's working groups who have expressed their views on the question of parliamentary government for the USSR have maintained that a balance can and should be struck between parliamentarianism and Lenin's original concept of the soviets by incorporating elements of each into a single project that is both congruent with Soviet historical traditions and political culture, and adequate to the tasks facing the USSR today.[52] Above all, in their view, parliamentarianism highlights the importance of transforming soviets into authentic working legislatures capable of directing the operations of government at all levels. In order to effect such a transformation, they go on to tap a number of institutional features commonly associated with the idea of parliamentary government.

First, the conventional method of selecting deputies to soviets on the basis of quotas issued by superior party organs that specify that a certain percentage of deputies should be industrial workers, a certain percentage, women, and so forth should be dropped. Real legislatures require competent legislators. Therefore, ability rather than socio-economic characteristics should be the sole criterion in choosing deputies. Along the same lines, a measure of professionalism would need to be introduced into legislative work. Deputies should be relieved of more of their regular employment obligations than has hitherto been the case in order to devote sufficient time to their legislative duties.

Second, proper legislation is produced by legislatures. The extant pattern, whereby legislative acts drawn up by the apparatus are routinely approved by a mass of uniformed deputies summoned for short occasions to endorse by acclamation the policies of others, must be terminated. Instead, the sessional activity of soviets should be extended over much longer periods, thus providing them with sufficient time to conduct their own legislative work. Toward that same end, the number of deputies in each soviet should be reduced to manageable proportions. Fewer, more knowledgeable deputies who devote their time to legislative work would represent a great advance in this respect over a mass of uninformed deputies who go through the motions of legislating—literally, raising their hands in approval at the appropriate moments—from time to time.

Finally, in order to guarantee the integrity of the legislative process, a division of legislative and executive power should be instituted. With regard to personnel, this division would prohibit administrative officials employed by a given soviet from serving as deputies to that same soviet. Moreover, executive and legislative institutions should be clearly distinguished by depriving executive committees, composed mainly of administrators, of their role as organizers and directors of soviet work and by awarding these functions to prezidiums of soviets which are composed exclusively (or almost exclusively) of their top legislative officers.[53] This institutional separation would not only lodge the leadership of the legislature where it belongs, with the legislators, but also enable this leadership to monitor the executive branch now organized as the administrative arm, rather than the head, of the soviet.[54]

The other general question addressed by the working groups, the democratization of Soviet electoral practices, has immediate implications for the introduction of limited parliamentary forms into the structure of government. If soviets are to function as autonomous institutions, then the monopoly on the selection of their deputies that has been enjoyed by the party apparatus must be broken. With that end in view, two members of the Prezidium's working group on amendments to the Constitution had published an important article on the eve of the Nineteenth Party Conference that presaged certain features of the electoral reform that were included in the final version of the project.[55] The nominations process should be opened up to citizens in their places of residence, they argued, in order to replace the prevailing system of 'administered democracy'—a reference to the party apparatus' control over the nominations process in the workplace—with an electoral system featuring genuine competition for office and real pluralism among contending candidates and programmes. Although these authors personally favoured the introduction of multiple candidates for each individual seat, they believed that the USSR was at the time 'not yet ready for one-to-one competition for office and its resulting division of contestants for office into winners and losers'.[56] Therefore, as a compromise step in the direction of competitive single-member district races, they advocated the formation of multi-seat districts with a plurality of candidates, along the model of the 1987 experimental elections.

The major compromises on electoral democracy written into the drafts of the Constitutional amendments and Electoral Law by the working groups, however, were compromises with the apparatus. These involved the creation of a multi-staged nominations process in which the apparatus could apply its influence at strategic points to weed out candidates that it might oppose, and the provision by which public organizations would name one-third of the deputies to every soviet. Since the party apparatus controlled most if not all of these public organizations internally, a robust representation of the apparatus in future soviets was thus ensured. Members of the working groups expected these provisions to be severely criticized by a considerable section of the Soviet public. Their expectations were, if anything, exceeded when the project was finally unveiled.

## NOTES

1.  The continuity between the Resolutions adopted by the Nineteenth Party Conference and the draft Constitutional amendments and Electoral Law was stressed repeatedly by advocates of the reform in both public meetings and newspaper articles. A clear statement of this alleged continuity can be found in Gorbachev's address to the session of the Supreme Soviet at which the measures became law. See the Report of M. S. Gorbachev, 'K polnovlastiyu Sovetov i sozidaniya sotsialisticheskogo pravovogo gosudarstvo', *Izvestiya* (3 Dec. 1988).
2.  M. Kushtapin, 'Kommissiya odobrila popravki i predlozheniya', *Izvestiya* (20 Nov. 1988); 'Deputaty golosuyut za popravki', *ibid.* (21 Nov. 1988). The TASS report on the drafts of the Constitutional amendments and the Electoral Law that were submitted to the Supreme Soviet for ratification claimed that 'the Soviet people see [in the drafts] a real implementation of the decisions of the Nineteenth All-Union Conference of the CPSU...'. See 'Zasedanie Prezidiuma Vekhovnogo Soveta SSSR', *ibid.* (28 Nov. 1988).
3.  G. P. Razumovskii's speech to the Twelfth Extraordinary Session of the Supreme Soviet of the USSR (1 Dec. 1988), *Izvestiya* (2 Dec. 1988).
4.  Gorbachev, 'K polnovlastiyu Sovetov ...'.
5.  See V. Vasil'ev's comments in the interview conducted by V. Khatyntsev, 'Zakonotvorchestvo', *Pravda* (7 Nov. 1988). The Commission for Legislative Proposals formed in the Central Committee of the CPSU to oversee the legislative project also seems to have played no appreciable role. It met to review the drafts of the amendments to the Constitution and the new Law on Elections a few days before these drafts were made public. According to TASS, the Commission simply endorsed the proposed legislative changes. See 'Zasedanie Komissii', *Izvestiya* (19 Oct. 1988).
6.  Accounts of the campaigns conducted during these competitive by-elections can be found in M. Morozov, 'Vybirali ... i ne vybirali', *Pravda* (28 Sept. 1988); A. Kondrashov and M. Kushtapin, 'Pochemu rabochii V. Korolev budet golosovat' protiv', *Izvestiya* (20 Oct. 1988).
7.  Eric F. Green, *The 19th Conference of the CPSU: Politics and Policy* (Washington, D.C.: American Committee on U.S.-Soviet Relations, 1988), pp. 7-10.

8.  Stephen White, 'Gorbachev, Gorbachevism, and the Party Conference', *The Journal of Communist Studies*, Vol. 4 (Dec., 1988), p. 151.
9.  A remarkable account outlining the methods employed by the party organs to control in every detail the conduct of soviet work can be found in Yu. V. Shabanov's *Partiinoe rukovodstvo Sovetami deputatov trudyashchikhsya* (Minsk: Belarus', 1969). The passage of this book through the state censorship assumedly owed something to its style. It introduces each aspect of party domination under phrases such as 'the electoral system in the USSR is the most democratic in the world' (p. 25) and then goes on to subvert such endorsements by recounting just how the apparatus dictates to soviets their every move—in this instance, precisely who will be 'elected' as deputies.
10. Interview (11 Oct. 1988). References to the party's ability to manipulate the outcomes of the experimental elections of 1987 can be found in the previous Chapter. On the by-elections of 1988, see V. Razboinikov, 'Demokratiya i demogogiya', *Izvestiya* (25 July 1988); S. Suslikov, 'Vsego odin kandidat', *ibid.* (5 Oct. 1988).
11. Z. Shevnina (Head of the Organization Dept., Sovetskii *raikom* of the CPSU, Moscow Oblast'), 'Informatsiya Sovetskogo raikoma KPSS ob organizatorskoi politicheskoi rabote po podgotovke k vyboram v mestnye Sovety narodnykh deputatov v usloviyakh eksperimenta' (mimeo; 11 June 1987).
12. A. Shutyleva, 'Spravka' (mimeo; no date, *circa* June 1987).
13. L. Osipov, V. Seleznev and O. Obukhov, 'Informatsiya o provedeniya vyborov v mestnye Sovety narodnykh deputatov i narodnykh sudei v Sovetskom raione', (mimeo; 21 June 1987).
14. L. Ponomarev and V. Shinkarenko, 'Dogmatizm: korni i krona', *Izvestiya* (10 June 1988).
15. L. Ponomarev and V. Shinkarenko, 'Kto kogo?', *Izvestiya* (19 May 1988).
16. *Ibid.*
17. In early 1988, the historian, Yu. N. Afanas'ev, reached a unique arrangement with a Soviet publishing house whereby a collection of political essays, contributed by some thirty-four Soviet intellectuals (all outspoken proponents of democratization) would be published without having to pass through any form of censorship. Afanas'ev's intention was to provide each delegate to the Nineteenth Party Conference with a copy of this tome. Before the Conference convened, however, Afanas'ev's book, *Inogo ne dano* (Moscow: Progress, 1988), was confiscated by certain elements in the apparatus reportedly acting under the authority of Politboro conservative, E. K. Ligachev. Copies of this book have subsequently turned up in foreign currency bookshops in Moscow.
18. Mikhail Gorbachev, 'On Progress in Implementing the Decisions of the 27th CPSU Congress and the Tasks of Promoting Perestroika', *19th All-Union Conference of the CPSU: Documents and Materials* (Moscow: Novosti, 1988), p. 51.
19. *Izvestiya* (1 July 1988).
20. See the speech of V. K. Belyaninov, secretary of the Moscow *gorkom*, *Izvestiya* (30 June 1988).
21. These remarks were made by A. M. Masaliev, First Secretary of the Communist Party of Kirgizia, *Izvestiya* (30 June 1988).
22. Gorbachev, 'On Progress in Implementing the Decisions of the 27th CPSU Congress...', pp. 42, 49.
23. For contending views on the subject, see the speeches by V. V. Bakatin and L. I. Albalkin, *Izvestiya* (30 June 1988), and that by I. D. Laptev, *ibid.* (1 July 1988).

24. Conversations that I had in Moscow during September and October of 1988 with journalists who cover soviet affairs and with a number of specialists in the field of state and law have led me to this conclusion. The impression that I received from these conversations was that the success of any or all of the other reform proposals hinged on the conditions under which these two offices would be combined. For examples of this controversy, see N. Nazorbaev, 'Razrubit' valovoi uzel', *Pravda* (9 July 1988); I. Shvets, 'Chto dast sovmeshchenie postov', *ibid.* (27 Sept. 1988); P. Prigornitskii, Letter to the Editor, *Izvestiya* (29 July 1988).

25. Boris Pavlovich Kurashvili, 'K polnovlastiyu Sovetov', *Kommunist*, No. 8 (May, 1988), pp. 28-30; esp., pp. 34-35. Shortly after the Party Conference, Kurashvili, perhaps with undue modesty, referred to Gorbachev's proposal to combine these offices as 'unexpected'. He then went on to elaborate on the wisdom of pursuing such a course. See his 'Sekretar' i predsedatel' v odnom litse', *Izvestiya* (22 July 1988).

26. Gorbachev, 'On Progress in Implementing the Decisions of the 27th Party Congress ...', p. 49.

27. *Ibid.*

28. *Ibid.*

29. 'Resolutions of the 19th All-Union Conference of the CPSU', *19th All-Union Conference of the CPSU: Documents and Materials*, p. 133.

30. *Ibid.*

31. *Ibid.*, p. 132.

32. *Ibid.*

33. *Ibid.*, pp. 157-158.

34. *Ibid.*, p. 158.

35. *Ibid.*

36. *Ibid.*, p. 118.

37. V. Prozorov, in an interview conducted by Yu. Feofanov, 'Ot proekta do zakona', *Izvestiya* (9 Dec. 1988). See also the remarks of V. Popov in an interview conducted by N. Volynskii, 'Vlast' Sovetov, vlast' naroda', *Pravda* (31 Oct. 1988).

38. The comment was made by I. N. Shumshin of the Academy of Science's Institute of State and Law and a deputy of a district soviet in Moscow at a constituents' meeting in the Brateevo micro-raion of Moscow that was called to discuss the draft amendments to the Constitution (18 Nov. 1988).

39. 'Zakonotvorchestvo', *Pravda* (7 Nov. 1988).

40. One example of such a disputed issue that was settled by the Politburo involved the Constitutional powers awarded to the President of the Supreme Soviet. In this instance, the Politburo, at Gorbachev's insistence, selected the 'weak' variant of Presidential power that the Prezidium's working group had drafted.

41. An instance in which 'Gorbachev's circle' dictated the precise content of the provisions that the working groups were to draft involved the designation of which public organizations were eligible to select deputies to the Congress of People's Deputies, the number of deputies allotted to each, and the method by which these deputies would be chosen. Two members of the working groups in question mentioned in interviews that their groups opposed these measures that emanated from Gorbachev's circle.

42. Interview (19 Oct. 1988).

43. Public meeting sponsored by the Political Club of the graduate students of the Law Faculty, Moscow State University (4 Nov. 1988). Similar statements were made by another member of one of the working groups during an interview (20 Oct. 1988). The minimalist and maximalist positions on

democratization that surfaced in the working groups appear to reflect the currents of political opinion in the larger society as described by B. P. Kurashvili in his 'Formula sotsializma', *Kommunist Estonii*. 5 (1989), pp. 12-23.

The minimalist position, what Kurashvili calls 'enlightened authoritarianism', relies in his view on catch-phrases such as 'what is really possible and achievable' to excuse its 'half-hearted [endorsement] of *perestroika*'. This shibboleth and others like it became arguments of last resort for supporters of the project when debating opponents during the nationwide assessment that began in late October. For an analysis very similar to that of Kurashvili, see G. Popov, 'Ten Theses on the Second Stage of Perestroika', *Glasnost*, Nos. 16-18 (Jan., 1989), pp. 48-49.

44.  V. I. Lenin, *State and Revolution* (Moscow: Progress, 1969).
45.  For a recent endorsement of this view, see A. Sergeev, 'Sovety i upravlenie ekonomikoi', *Sovety narodnykh deputatov* , (July, 1988), pp. 41-44.
46.  These views were stated forcefully, and greeted with enthusiastic and prolonged applause, by individuals such as G. N. Gurili, leader of the informal political organization, the Avenir Nozarin Union of Soviet Popular Sovereignty, and M. S. Aivagyan, Senior Research Associate at the Academy of Science's Institute of State and Law, at public debates on the proposed Constitutional amendments that took place in Moscow in November of 1988.
47.  This comment was made in conversation by a senior Soviet legal specialist who was closely connected with a number of the members of the Prezidium's working groups (21 Oct. 1988). It was typical of numerous such statements made by other specialists with whom I spoke.
48.  Kurashvili, 'K polnovlastiyu Sovetov'; Fedor Burlatskii, 'O sovetskom parlamentarizme', *Literaturnaya gazeta* (15 June 1988), p. 2.
49.  Both Kurashvili and Burlatskii were also reported to be directly associated with Gorbachev's circle.
50.  B. P. Kurashvili, 'Kakoi byt' strukture vlasti?', *Izvestiya* (28 July 1988).
51.  B. P. Kurashvili, 'Verkhovnaya vlast': iz proshlogo v budushchee', *Izvestiya* (15 Nov. 1988).
52.  G. V. Barabashev, V. I. Vasil'ev and K. F. Sheremet, 'Sovety narodnykh deputatov', *Sovetskoe gosudarstvo i pravo*, No. 5 (May, 1988), pp. 3-13.
53.  The formation of such a prezidium has already been carried out by some local soviets, reports S. I. Shishkin, with positive results. See his, *Kraevoi, oblastnoi Sovet: problemy kompleksnogo razvitiya territorii* (Irkutsk: Irkutsk University, 1988), p. 105. See also L. Oborkina, 'Sovetu—reshat', ispolkomu—ispolnyat''', *Sovety narodnykh deputatov*, (July, 1988), pp. 9-10.
54.  Since under the Soviet administrative principle of 'dual subordination' the administrative departments of a given soviet are responsible to both that soviet and to their equivalent departments organized under the soviet at the level above them, the creation of a prezidium *per se* does not ensure legislative control of the executive branch at a given level. Administrative departments can sidestep the control of their respective prezidium on the basis of directives issued by their supervisors in the administrative hierarchy. For this reason, members of the working groups have advocated adjustments in the principle of dual subordination in order to reduce the influence of administrative bodies and increase that of legislative ones. Adjustments in this area, however, would pose a threat to the centralized system of administration on which the power of the apparatus is based. Perhaps for this reason, the question of the future of dual subordination has not been addressed in specifics. For the thoughts of three members of Prezidium's working groups on this

issue, see Barabashev, Vasil'ev and Sheremet, 'Sovety narodnykh deputatov', p. 12.
55.  G. V. Barabashev and K. F. Sheremet, 'Sovetskaya izbiratel'naya sistema: strategiya reformy', *Kommunist*, No. 9  (June, 1988), pp. 23-30.
56.  Interview with G. V. Barabashev (9 May 1989).

# 4. THE PROJECT ASSESSED AND DEBATED

## THE NATIONWIDE ASSESSMENT AND THE PUBLIC DEBATE

The nationwide assessment officially commenced with the publication of the draft amendments to the Constitution on 22 October and, on the following day, the draft of the new Electoral Law in all the national newspapers of the USSR. Over the ensuing month, individual citizens, public officials, legal specialists, labour collectives and 'informal' political groups engaged in a wide-ranging and sometimes intense debate on the various measures contained in the drafts. These phenomena, nationwide assessment and public debate, were not, however, one and the same. The difference between them does not so much concern the participants or the arguments that they advanced on any particular aspect of the legislative project. Differences in these respects were apparent, but they were neither so great nor so clear-cut as to divide in two these concurrent processes. Rather, what distinguished the nationwide assessment from the public debate was the fact that the authorities orchestrated the former in order to produce a predetermined result—namely, the appearance of public consultation and approval—while they simply permitted the latter to take place and run its own freewheeling course. Consequently, the nationwide assessment comprised an integral part of the political reform conceived and ultimately implemented by the authorities. Its parameters were more or less fixed and its outcome never in doubt. In contrast, the public debate that occurred alongside it was spontaneous. It was an opportunity for citizens to express themselves freely on the legislative project that the authorities had prepared. It established its own parameters in the course of discussion, which was usually face-to-face, and arrived at no final result other than a general apprehension that the project was deeply flawed and that the period of nationwide assessment should be extended in order to debate the matter more.

With this distinction in mind, we might frame our discussion of the draft proposals and the public's reaction to them by examining how the process of nationwide assessment was structured by the authorities. By situating the nationwide assessment in the context of democratization from above, we can consider how it, like other moments in the reform process, was shaped by contradiction. From this vantage, we notice a regime relying on a well established political ritual in order to midwife its project of instituting a radically new political order. As in the past, the regime would go through the motions of submitting its proposals to the public for their consideration. As in the past, the public could not, in the end, reject the proposals. Approval was either assumed or regarded as a matter of no particular relevance. V. G. Lomonsov, chairperson of the Supreme Soviet's subcommission that was formed to review and respond to public comment on the drafts, admitted as much himself in remarking that:

> There is nothing strange in the [proposed] amendments [to the Constitution]. They have been worked out on the basis of the decisions of the [Nineteenth Party] Conference and have therefore already passed the test of public opinion.[1]

In certain respects, then, this nationwide assessment was a repeat of those that had gone before. Like its predecessors, it would generate hundreds of thousands of public comments and suggestions that would effectively be ignored by those to whom they were addressed.[2]

In other respects, however, there was something new about this assessment because there was indeed something new about the project itself. In the words of R. F. Vasil'ev, a member of the Prezidium's working group on the Electoral Law, the 'Constitution of 1977 was a fake'. It changed nothing in political life because it was not a Constitution at all, just an empty document that boasted about the alleged achievements of the USSR in constructing socialism.[3] The current project was of a different order. The political authorities were now in some way serious about changing political life. The process by which this change was to come about must to some extent reflect the seriousness of that commitment if it were, in turn, to be taken seriously enough by the public to engender the popular participation on which the ultimate success of the project itself would depend. The relative openness of the mass media to criticisms of the project, at least when compared with previous exercises of this type, and the unrestricted scope of discussion tolerated in the public debate count as indications that the regime was not simply staging another charade. But if it was prepared to permit society some voice, it was not at the same time pledging that this voice would have the final say. Indeed, the fact that only one month was allotted for public discussion of the new project, whereas the adoption of the 'fake' Constitution of 1977 was preceded by some six months of (equally fake) nationwide assessment, would suggest a sort of inverse relationship between time and substance. Since this legislative project represented more than merely another collection of fine words, since it intended a real opening toward democracy, then the public would be entitled to its say. But it had to be quick about it.

A number of equally contradictory aspects of the nationwide assessment appear in the design of the organizational machinery that was established to review and respond to the views expressed by the public. On the formal side, the main gear of this machinery was a 10-member 'preparatory' subcommission formed on 25 October by the Supreme Soviet's 66-member Joint Commission on Legislative Proposals. The subcommission enlisted the aid of the legal specialists from the working groups who had composed the drafts. Throughout the assessment period, the subcommission met to review the criticisms and suggestions that arrived in the form of letters, telegrams and phone calls to government offices, party committees and the mass media. On the basis of this review, it introduced a number of modifications and corrections into the drafts and forwarded these to the Joint Commission of Legislative Proposals that submitted the amended drafts to the Supreme Soviet for ratification. These formal arrangements were evidently intended to highlight the fact that the assessment process was conducted in accordance with strict legal procedures and oriented toward taking an attentive and fair account of public opinion. In the words of one commentator:

> There are practically no articles in the drafts that would not go through the all-people's expertise, that the specialists [from the working groups] would not again try to rethink by taking into account the most varied opinions and proposals.[4]

The actual structure of working relations, however, was quite the reverse of the formal one. In order to appreciate the degree to which the reality of the nationwide assessment departed from its idealized representation, we might work our way upwards from the grassroots, where the letters and so forth were composed, to the corridors of power where they were reviewed and acted on. In so doing, we note, first, that the apparatus in the localities conducted an extensive campaign designed to demonstrate that the legislative drafts enjoyed the full support of the great majority of the population. To this end, meetings of labour collectives were convened for the purpose of affixing signatures to 'collective letters' that endorsed in full the proposed legal changes.[5] In some places, members of the apparatus mass-produced form letters that individuals were requested to sign and mail in themselves.[6] At the top, the Propaganda Department of the Central Committee issued instructions, according to certain Soviet journalists, that set boundaries on what sorts of critical letters the newspapers were allowed to print and what limits should be observed by their own writers in commenting on the legislative project. Perhaps the most distinguished casualty in this struggle over the printed word was Moskovskaya tribuna (Moscow Tribune), a discussion club that was formed on 12 October by many of the same individuals—Yurii Afanas'ev, Ales Adamovich, Andrei Sakharov, Yurii Burtin, Tatyana Zaslavskaya and others—who had earlier authored the uncensored and ultimately confiscated collection of political essays, *Inogo ne dano*, mentioned above. Announcing themselves as a 'constructive opposition' for reform, the 100 or so members of Moskovskaya tribuna sent a letter containing their criticisms of the legislative drafts to the USSR's major newspapers, but none would publish it. Although this group of leading Soviet intellectuals did participate in the public debate, they were denied a role in the nationwide assessment.

The Prezidium of the Supreme Soviet was the ultimate destination for all comment on the drafts generated by the nationwide assessment. Members of the Prezidium's apparatus received and catalogued over 300,000 letters that were directly addressed to the Prezidium itself[7] and also monitored all national and many republic-level newspapers, television and radio broadcasts for comment that they carried on the legislative project. The sheer volume of this material would raise obvious questions regarding the ability of any organization to deal with it effectively in the space of a month. The image projected by the authorities, however, attempted to correlate volume with effect, to associate magically, as it were, the mountain of mail with the idea that it represented a genuine popular influence on the final version of the project adopted by the Supreme Soviet.[8] But the qualitative determinations made by the Prezidium's staff that handled the letters had a greater bearing on the assessment process than did the sheer quantity of mail itself.

The Prezidium's staff prepared daily synopses of public comment in two editions (one pertaining to the draft amendments to the Constitution, the other to the draft of the Electoral Law), and forwarded these to the specialists from the working groups who were formally assisting the preparatory subcommission of the Supreme Soviet's Joint Commission on Legislative Proposals. Judging from three of these synopses that I have read, the Prezidium's staff engaged in some rather heavy editing. The first collection, dated 3 November 1988, covered 190 pages and included some 700 individual items[9], most of which were either blanket endorsements of the draft proposals or minor criticisms intended to clarify the language of the drafts. A small number of these items (seven by my reckoning) concerned issues of more substance, but none addressed the two points most vigorously argued in the public debate—the selection of deputies by public organizations and the role of electoral commissions and pre-electoral district meetings in the nominations process.[10] The sharpest criticisms included in this report came from members of the Estonian Popular Front (two items), yet the way in which the editors had rendered each tended to characterize, if not caricaturize, it as a narrowly nationalist complaint that was out of step with public opinion in general. The other two synopses that I read appeared on 15 November and were of slightly greater length.[11] Both contained a larger number of serious criticisms than did the synopsis of 3 November and included clear references to the contentious issues regarding the role of public organizations, electoral commissions and pre-electoral district meetings that had been absent from the earlier report. But at this juncture, time was already becoming an important factor. Indeed, on the very day that this report appeared, the Prezidium's staff also issued another long document[12] that listed nearly every modification that was eventually introduced into the final drafts of the legislative project.[13]

A related question that concerned the impact of public comment on the legislative project involved the role of the various actors who worked with the materials that had been prepared by the Prezidium's staff. Although the specialists from the working groups were, in principle, merely assisting the preparatory subcommission, the available evidence would indicate that they in fact directed its deliberations and authored various recommendations made in its name. The specialists from the working groups convened on an almost daily basis during the nationwide assessment in order to go over the synopses of public comment that the Prezidium's staff had produced. A. I. Luk'yanov, who had been named Vice-President of the Supreme Soviet on 1 October, attended many of these meetings and played a direct role in deciding which sections of the drafts would be modified and what specific changes would be incorporated in the final versions. In contrast, the subcommission, which did not even hold its first meeting until half of the assessment period had elapsed[14], found itself in the role of reviewing various recommendations and proposed changes that Luk'yanov's legal specialists (the subcommission's 'advisers') had already set out in detail. The legal specialists with whom I spoke regarded the subcommission as a purely formal body that played no autonomous part in the process of preparing the final drafts of the legislative project. As one specialist candidly remarked, 'the members of the subcommission are stupid, they have no juridical training and they accept whatever we tell them'.[15]

A final question that might be raised about the role of the legal specialists in responding to public comment and introducing appropriate revisions into the legislative drafts concerns the authenticity of the process itself. For example, V. Vasil'ev, one of Luk'yanov's group, gave an interview to a *Pravda* correspondent in which he stressed the outstanding credentials of the legal specialists working on the project. After outlining the way in which their work was organized, he went on to provide an illustration of how the suggestions coming in from the public had enabled the specialists to improve the draft legislation. The case he cited involved the issue of rotating deputies through the Supreme Soviet. In the draft of the Constitutional amendments promulgated for nationwide assessment, there was a provision whereby 'up to one-fifth' of the deputies on the Supreme Soviet would be replaced annually. Vasil'ev mentioned in this respect a letter that had arrived from a seamstress in the Crimea that pointed out the imprecision of this wording. 'Up to one-fifth' could, after all, be interpreted to mean far fewer than one-fifth of the members. According to Vasil'ev's account, fifteen doctors and candidates of law thought over and discussed the seamstress' recommendation and 'agreed unanimously...[to adopt] the

proposal "not less than one-fifth" [which] is more precise'.[16] Although
Vasil'ev's account was apparently intended to demonstrate that ordinary citizens were taking an active and influential part in the nationwide
assessment, the revisions made in the final draft of this article in fact
had nothing to do with the seamstress. Rather, the authors of the
legislation deliberately included in this case, and in some others,[17]
certain provisions in the initial draft that they fully intended to change
in the final version. The tactic was to present to the public these
unwanted provisions in the expectation that they would elicit criticism,
and then to introduce revisions that had already been planned by the
authors under the guise of responding to public comment.

In the end, the nationwide assessment accomplished very little in
the sense of persuading, much less compelling, the authorities to alter
anything of substance in the drafts. Like the legislative project itself,
the process of nationwide assessment belonged more to the authorities
than to the public. Yet it would be mistaken to regard it as merely an
exercise orchestrated by the powerful that was designed to throw a cloak
of legitimacy around what from start to finish remained their project.
For the project and, of course, the assessment of it provided opportunities for citizens to act. Certainly the opportunities were limited, but
their presence distinguished this project and this assessment from all
those that had gone before. As Gorbachev remarked in his address to
the Supreme Soviet convened to ratify the new legislation:

> The fact that support for the draft laws was this time not purely formal is
> of importance as well. On the contrary, their publication gave rise to an
> active exchange of views, lively discussions, and a multitude of various
> suggestions and amendments.[18]

Although the overwhelming majority of these suggestions and
amendments had no significant impact on the project, it does not follow
that the nationwide assessment was itself without significance. During
the early stage of the process, for instance, *Izvestiya* reported on the
many telephone calls that it was receiving from interested citizens and
drew particular attention to the caller's tone of voice. If in the past the
public had been content to have 'a consultative voice', the newspaper
explained, today it has acquired 'the intonation of the deciding voice.
People no longer want laws that are bestowed on them from above.
They long to create for themselves the limits between the permitted and

the restricted'.[19] As the assessment completed its final stage, *Izvestiya* characterized this aspect of the process as:

> the first and extraordinarily important result of this unusually saturated and intense month [of nationwide assessment]—a clearly palpable surmounting of the political inertia of society, the growth of the civic activity of the Soviet people.[20]

In its own peculiar way, then, the nationwide assessment succeeded as a critical stage in the transition to a democratic order. Even those who in the public debates expressed complete opposition to the legislative project were nonetheless participating in this transition. Moreover, it represented for them an opportunity to speak their minds, to argue their views; to act, in short, as citizens. In this respect, the nationwide assessment and its orphan child, the public debate, were something of a rehearsal for a citizens' politics that would soon emerge in the course of the election campaigns.

## ASSESSMENT AND DEBATE IN POLITICAL FOCUS

We exclude from our analysis of public comment on the legislative project the great bulk of letters and articles on this topic that appeared in the press.[21] According to *Pravda* and *Izvestiya* most letters that reached their respective editorial offices were either unreserved endorsements of the published drafts or suggestions aimed at improving them.[22] A letter from a certain I. Vorob'ev of the Moscow region was perhaps representative of the first type. 'I warmly endorse', his letter read,

> the legislative project that has been published. I am very glad that for our party the word has not parted company with the deed. The law must now only be strictly observed in order for us actively to be helping *perestroika*.[23]

Along the lines of the second pattern, we find those published comments aimed at improving the wording of the drafts by removing lexical imprecisions and ambiguities. Accordingly, letters of this type complained about phrases such as 'as a rule' that appeared in the initial drafts in reference to whether ballots would include more candidates than there are seats under contention; or, as in the case of our Crimean seamstress, the expression 'up to one-fifth' with respect to the number of deputies on the Supreme Soviet who would be replaced annually.

There are a number of reasons for excising these two sorts of comment from our study. First, as noted above, much of the unabashed approval that the press received was manufactured by the apparatus. Even in those instances in which it may not have been, it is very difficult to interpret what the approvers were approving. Given the fact that the Constitution that was in the process of being amended was formally more democratic than the amendments under discussion, should simple approval of the project be interpreted as disapproval of democratic institutions? Or did the authors have something else in mind, something along the lines of what G. N. Gurili argued before a public meeting during the period of nationwide assessment? 'The old Constitution', he remarked, 'was more democratic, but this new one will give real power to the soviets and they will begin to act, little by little, democratically'.[24] Unfortunately, we simply have no way to ascertain which of the blanket endorsements were indeed genuinely put forward by individuals; even if we did, we still could not accurately interpret the meaning(s) of these endorsements because of the ambiguity that results from the absence of context. Has a given writer signified his approval of the project because he wishes to endorse the restrictions on democracy introduced into the letter of the law, or because he regards the spirit of the project as one likely to engender real democratic practices?

A second reason for excluding these two patterns of comment from our discussion involves the constraints imposed upon the press as we noted in the preceding section of this chapter. Consider the words of a participant in the public debate on the project who wondered out loud, 'Who sends these letters to the press and what is their real content?'[25] We do not want to reinforce the characterizations lent to the nationwide assessment by a press operating under political constraints.

Finally, although a number of the suggested improvements were advanced by way of political argument, some questions remain with respect to the content of the initial drafts and, therefore, the status of the suggested improvements themselves. P. D'yachenko, for example, wrote to *Pravda* complaining about the phrase, 'as a rule', that appeared in Article 100 of the initial draft. D'yachenko pointed out that a document that called for more candidates than seats under contention, and employed the phrase 'as a rule' in this regard, would leave the door open to the apparatus to stage single-candidate elections in those districts where they found themselves unable to prevent the nomination of individuals whom they did not approve.[26] Although letters of this type clearly register the political views of their authors, they may well belong to the category that includes our Crimean seamstress; namely, statements that take issue with what the framers of the legislative project wrote which would then be appropriated by the authorities who, under the pretense of responding to public opinion, introduce those changes in the final drafts that they had in mind from the start. Having no desire to participate in this chicanery ourselves, we consequently exclude from our discussion this category of popular proposals.

Where do these excisions then leave us? In a word, with the public debate and a rump of the nationwide assessment that expressed varying degrees of opposition to the legislative project on the basis of democratic principles. These currents of opinion were especially troublesome for defenders of the project who regularly employed the language of democracy to characterize the expected transfer of power from administrative and party bodies to the soviets. For, in so doing, they found themselves at a double disadvantage *vis-à-vis* opponents of the project who criticized the drafts from a democratic perspective. Not only had supporters, in order to legitimate the project, set in motion a discourse on democracy in general terms that opponents could turn against them by pointing to the undemocratic features of this same project; but the medium of democratization itself—the series of Constitutional amendments under consideration—necessarily invited comparisons with those provisions of the existing Constitution that were scheduled for alteration, provisions which, in a formal sense, were more democratic than the proposed amendments. Critics, when measuring the drafts against either democratic principles or the contents of the Constitution in place, invariably regarded the project as a 'disappointment', a 'departure from the principles endorsed at the Nineteenth Party Conference', a 'step backward', even in some cases as an 'anti-democratic project' or a 'counter-revolutionary coup'.[27] Supporters, in reply, could do little more than state in the most general terms that the project was simply the extension of what had been approved at the Nineteenth Party Conference or resort to vague constructions such as 'overall, it represents a step forward'.[28]

Those authors of the legislative project who defended it at public meetings or in newspaper articles were perhaps especially hard-pressed to formulate convincing replies to their critics. Painfully aware of the political accommodation with the apparatus that undergirded the project, they were at the same time unable to introduce it openly into discussion for fear of undoing the accommodation itself. As a consequence, they often oscillated between two, quite inconsistent, modes of argumentation. One referred to an expansion of democracy that they alleged to be contained in the legislative project, the other amounted to putting on the poor mouth in order to elicit patience and understanding from their audience. 'It is only a first step', some would say (in other words, 'please be patient'); 'of course, it is not perfect', others would add (in other words, 'please understand that this is the best thing we can do under present circumstances').[29] These ellipses issued from the fact that the reference required to complete the logic of their arguments— 'you must realize that the authorities are at this point prepared to introduce this much real democracy and no more'—was precisely the one that circumstances forbade them to make. And absent this reference, much of the nationwide assessment and public debate that occurred necessarily amounted to an exercise in which both proponents and opponents of the legislative project would spend the greater portion of their energies talking past one another.

## MAJOR POINTS OF CONTENTION

It remains here to outline the critical points of argument that emerged during the nationwide assessment. Our discussion of these is organized around the key provisions contained in the legislative project as set out earlier in Chapter 1. Accordingly, we begin with those changes in the law that bear on the electoral system.

*Nominations and Elections.* Some of the heaviest criticisms levelled at the legislative project concerned the provision whereby a third of the deputies to all soviets would be selected by public organizations. How can we use the term 'people's deputies' [*narodnye deputaty*], wondered one critic, when these individuals have not been elected by the people?[30] In public debates, speakers often referred to this provision as a throwback to a type of feudal arrangement in which society has been ordered into various estates, thereby eclipsing the very ideas of citizenship and equality upon which any conception of democracy must rest.[31] To many, the hand of the apparatus was obviously behind this measure. 'It is simply a clandestine method to continue party rule', said one. Another added that the 'so-called "public organizations" are really organs of state power, and this plan represents a cruel and deceitful step backward'.[32] 'It is foolish to think that these deputies will be in any way elected within the public organizations, they will be chosen by the ruling apparatus in each case.'[33] From the pamphlets distributed by 'informal' political groups[34] to a memorandum sent by the Supreme Court of the USSR to the Joint Commission on Legislative Proposals of the Supreme Soviet,[35] the idea that this method of selecting popular representatives had anything to do with advancing democracy was criticized and, indeed, ridiculed.

Most of the comment that appeared in the press on this matter trivialized the issue of fair representation. That is, the questionable aspects of the plan for public organizations to name their own deputies was usually reduced to the matter of unequal voting in which some citizens, who happened to be members of, say, the Central Committee of the Communist Party, would not only be able to vote in the popular elections along with everyone else, but would also enjoy another vote because of the deputies allotted by the project to their respective organizations.[36] The one exception that appeared during the nationwide assessment was an article by M. Chulaki, a Leningrad writer, who calculated that the system of selection by public organizations meant not one extra vote for the powerful, but thousands of extra votes. Chulaki observed that even if a full Congress of the CPSU were summoned to choose the 100 deputies apportioned to the party, the influence of each delegate in determining the final composition of the Congress of People's Deputies would be 6,000 times that of an ordinary citizen voting in the popular elections. Moreover, he noted, this would not only be true for certain members of the other public organizations, but a handful of individuals could end up with 12,000 or even 18,000 times the influence of common citizens if, for instance, they happened to be elected as delegates to the congresses of women's or veterans' societies as well. Poignantly, he concluded, 'even the old English lords only voted twice'.[37]

One of the authors of the project, Professor G. V. Barabashev of Moscow State University, was invited by the same newspaper to contribute a reply that was run alongside Chulaki's article.[38] Barabashev, who understood the project to contain two different principles of representation, one based on popular elections and the other on membership in public organizations, was constrained by his role to disregard this distinction and defend the project simply from the standpoint of representation in general.[39] Consequently, he produced a weak and unconvincing defense. Instead of addressing the magnitude of the differentials in the weights assigned to different classes of voters that Chulaki had pointed out, he side-stepped the issue by referring to the fact that whereas most voters in the USSR have been able, under existing law, to vote for two deputies to the Supreme Soviet (one in a territorial constituency and another in a national-territorial district), those residing in autonomous oblasts and okrugs have been able to vote for a third deputy who represented their respective region. Yet no one had ever complained about this inequality. Besides, he continued, direct elections, as advocated by opponents of the provision in question, have not produced democracy in the USSR but have served as a façade for the dominance of command-administrative bodies in political life. As Barabashev's rejoinder might suggest, since supporters of the project, because of contraints associated with the larger political accommodation, were required to keep silent on the central issue here, they could do little more than tiptoe around the problem, spinning sophistries and obfuscations.[40]

A strong consensus was apparent among participants in the nationwide assessment and public debate on the matter of introducing across-the-board competition in the general elections. As such, the procedures for nominating candidates, as outlined in the draft legislation, drew considerable fire from critics. At issue in this respect was an overriding concern that the party apparatus would retain its ability to control nominations and thus foreclose the possiblity of genuine elections.

This concern was expressed in a variety of ways. Sometimes participants in public debates would establish their credentials before their audience with comments such as 'I am not a member of the party, I haven't foresaken the people'.[41] On other occasions, party members, such as Professor A. A. Mishin of Moscow State University, warned that the nominations procedures in the draft legislation did nothing to prevent 'the dictatorship of the party apparatus' from manipulating the process in such a way as to confine electoral competition to a field of its hand-picked candidates.[42] In this regard, critics noted that the nomination of candidates at factory assemblies, usually attended by a handful of party officials and management personnel, would guarantee the selection of candidates beholden to the apparatus.[43]

The role of electoral commissions in the nominations process incited the suspicions of a number of participants in both the nationwide assessment[44] and public debate. What would ensure that the names of popular candidates who had been put forward at voters' meetings in their places of residence, or at meetings of labour collectives, would ultimately be placed on the ballot by the local electoral commissions? And the provision by which the electoral commissions can stage pre-electoral district meetings to reduce the number of nominees—was not this merely a convenient 'filter' for the apparatus, a way to eliminate those candidates that it did not approve while hiding its actions behind a psuedo-democratic smokescreen? In short, many critics felt, this mechanism would enable the apparatus to hijack the nominations process and, thereby, the elections themselves.[45] Boris Kagarlitskii, a prominent activist in the USSR's 'informal' political movement, seemed to sum up the opinions of many on this score with the remark that 'since the electoral commissions can refuse to register candidates, they are more sovereign than the people, and this is nonsense, this is absurd'.[46]

*The New Legislature.* 'Who needs this Congress?' queried one speaker in a public discussion of the draft legislation.[47] Her simple question was, in fact, a *double entendre* that encapsulated what many critics of the project saw as another filter designed to limit, if not prevent, popular control of government. On the one hand, this line of criticism ran, '*we* don't need it!' It is a 'far-fetched, artificial organ'[48] reminiscent of our experience with make-believe legislatures rather than the authentic parliament that we have been promised.[49] Moreover, since the Congress will be doing no more than selecting a working legislature (the Supreme Soviet) and a President, and then briefly reviewing their work once a year, a 'paradoxical situation [results] in which the majority of the voters are not represented in the real legislative organ'.[50] Authors of the project could do nothing to answer these objections except to refer either to the provisions of the Constitutional amendments which formally award power to the Congress[51] or to the 'Leninist tradition' of including amateurs in the affairs of state.[52]

On the other hand, this line of criticism continued, '*they* need it'. Many participants in the nationwide assessment regarded the Congress as a 'buffer' between the population and the real organs of power.[53] They expressed the fear that the Congress would essentially amount to a brief gathering of strangers, ignorant of each other's political programmes, that would not so much elect a Supreme Soviet as provide a veneer of democracy for an appointments process that remained firmly in the hands of the apparatus.[54] The provision whereby 20 per cent of the membership of the Supreme Soviet would rotate every year only compounded these concerns. Was this yet not another means by which the apparatus could maintain its dominant position, picking off those whom it found difficult to control and replacing them with more compliant souls? Indeed, the very existence of this procedure for turnover would encourage any independently-minded deputy who had managed to be elected to the Supreme Soviet to restrain himself for fear of rapidly ending his career as a legislator.[55]

*The President.* The critical commentary registered in the nationwide assessment on the draft amendments that pertained to the office of President of the Supreme Soviet tended to focus on the method by which he would be selected.[56] M. Chulaki argued that the same capacity for mischief that was built into the procedures for choosing the Supreme Soviet applied as well to the selection of the President. Ergo, like some participants in the public debate,[57] he called for equal and direct national elections to fill the post.[58]

Legal scholar, B. Gabrichidze, proposed another tack, namely, retaining the idea of electing the President from within the legislature, but ensuring his accountability by requiring that legislatures at all levels elect their chief officer on a competitive basis.[59] Gabrichidze's concern was in part fuelled by the understanding reached at the Nineteenth Party Conference that party committees would hereafter nominate, as a rule, their first secretaries to fill the position of president of the soviet at their corresponding levels of organization. This combination of offices would concentrate tremendous power in one pair of hands at each level of government and should therefore be checked by some mechanism of popular control. This same combination of offices, moreover, led a number of participants in the public debate to reject outright the idea of a President as outlined in the draft amendment.[60] 'Here we have,' said one, 'a tendency toward tyranny and the cult of personality'.[61] 'What is this', asked another, 'but a new dictator?'[62] 'This President will be less constrained than [Chilean dictator] Pinochet', argued a third, 'for here we have only one party'.[63] It should be added in this respect that these statements were greeted on each occasion by enthusiastic applause from those assembled. In some instances, subsequent speakers would make the point that, after all, Gorbachev will fill this new office and he is a man who can be trusted. But the modicum of uneasy assent that this argument elicited from the audience would rather quickly dissipate when another would mount the rostrum to remind the participants of their common experience of powerful rulers and the danger of 'yet another dictatorship' that the proposed amendments contained.[64]

*The Courts.* Two aspects of the proposed amendments to the Constitution that related to the judiciary became matters of intense concern to many critics of the project. The first, featured in the nationwide assessment, involved the questions of the independence of the courts and the departure taken in the draft amendment from the resolution adopted at the Nineteenth Party Conference that had called for the appointment of judges to lower courts by soviets at higher levels. Although there was considerable discussion in the press on this issue,[65] its effect, as noted above, was simply to encourage the authorities to do what they had planned from the beginning, namely, to drop the bogus proposal that would have had judges in local courts appointed by their corresponding soviets in favour of the resolution taken at the Party Conference.

The second aspect of the proposed amendments pertinent to the judiciary that aroused great concern involved an absence. A number of individuals had hoped that the proposed amendments would include provision for a Constitutional Court that would adjudicate fundamental questions of legality. Others, as the Supreme Court of the USSR stated in its memorandum to the Joint Commission on Legislative Proposals, believed that at a minimum the powers of the Supreme Court of the USSR and its counterparts in the union republics should be expanded so that these bodies could consider administrative regulations and legislative acts which were thought to violate the Constitution. Without a mechanism for upholding the fundamental law, critics complained, the idea of *pravovoe gosudarstvo*, a government based on the rule of law, would come to naught.[66] Defenders of the project pointed to the proposed Committee of Constitutional Oversight as an institution that, if properly organized, could accomplish the same ends, but many participants in the public debate, and even some in the nationwide assessment, did not regard it as an adequate substitute.[67] Ironically, although the initial draft of this amendment was modified in the final version, this was not done for reasons of legality and constitutionalism. Rather, the expansion of the size of the Committee of Constitutional Oversight from 15 to 23 members, and the addition of the stipulation that it must include at least one member from each of the union republics, were undertaken with the obvious intention of mollifying the intense opposition to the legislative project that had mounted in the Baltic republics.

*Federal Relations.* Under somewhat differing circumstances and at various rates of speed, popular movements aimed at autonomy, if not independence, for their respective republics emerged in Estonia, Latvia and Lithuania during the spring and summer of 1988. By the time these movements had been officially chartered in the autumn, it had become clear that the power of the Communist Party in each of these republics was exercised under licence from its respective 'popular front' (known in Lithuania as Sajudis).[68] The programmes of the popular fronts were grounded on the idea that each republic should be free from the control of the centre to solve its own problems and manage its own affairs. Economically, this meant that ownership of all land, resources and means of production must be in the hands of the republics.[69] Politically, it implied the right to reject directives from Moscow.[70]

The publication of the drafts of the legislative project was greeted in the Baltic with a storm of protest. Already the hitherto docile institutions of the party-state in these republics had begun to assert a measure of opposition to those announced policies of Moscow that were regarded as intrusions upon the rights of the republics.[71] But when the legislative project was unveiled, this opposition turned to outright rejection and produced a political crisis that took the authorities by surprise.

The basic objection aired in the Baltic to the proposed Constitutional amendments was summed up by V. Pakalniskis, Dean of the Law Faculty of Vilnius University: 'In these proposals, federalism is lost'.[72] On the one hand, critics argued, the project failed to guarantee equal representation for the republics on the Council of Nationalities of the Supreme Soviet, owing to the seats allocated to autonomous republics and regions which would swell out of all proportion the contingent of deputies representing, in particular, the Russian Republic on whose territory most of these units are located. Additionally, they continued, there is nothing in the project to ensure genuine representation for the republics on either chamber of the Supreme Soviet. Since the full Congress, not the republic, would be voting on whom to send to the real legislature, it might decide to fill the seats allotted to a given republic with deputies seleted by one of the public organizations rather than with those who enjoyed the support of that republic's citizens.[73]

On the other hand, the project was seen to provide no protection for the autonomy of the republics because it empowered the Congress of People's Deputies in Moscow to annul laws passed by republic legislatures. The movement to recapture an authentic national identity based on the practical reality of self-rule was feared hostage to the whim of strangers, ignorant of conditions in the Baltic, yet able to determine from afar the course of future events there.[74] Indeed, the fact that the proposed amendments mandated a structure of government for each of the republics that replicated in miniature that of the national government was regarded as ample indication of Moscow's insensitivity to the union republics' aspirations for a measure of genuine self determination.[75]

The popular movements in the Baltic challenged the Constitutional project on three fronts. One involved the citizens of the respective republics in a petition drive which called on the authorities to withdraw the project altogether. In the space of a week, organizers gathered some 720,000 signatures in Latvia, 861,000 in Estonia and 1.8 million in Lithuania. The enthusiastic response of the citizens in the Baltic to this rejectionist petition led one prominent activist to remark: 'This was more than a petition, it was a referendum.'[76]

A second front was mapped out at a meeting in Riga in early November attended by representatives from each of the popular fronts. Here, a common programme was worked out regarding the draft amendments to the Constitution, and the decision was taken to let the Estonians present it to Moscow. A telegram to Gorbachev resulted in his inviting the Estonians to appear before the preparatory subcommission of the Supreme Soviet's Joint Commission on Legislative Proposals that was monitoring the nationwide assessment. Subsequently, an Estonian delegation consisting of the President of the Estonian Supreme Soviet (A. F. Ruutel), a secretary of the Central Committee of the Communist Party of Estonia (Indrek Toome) and the President of the Estonian Popular Front (Marju Lauristin) repaired to Moscow and met with the preparatory subcommission on 9 November.

The meeting was a debate. The central authorities had invited to this gathering a number of leading officials from other union republics

whose presence seemed intended to impress upon the Estonians the idea
that their programme represented only a tiny minority out of step with
the rest of the country. Accordingly, the Estonians' request to shelve
the project was greeted with a counter-request from the subcommission
to shelve their objections to it.[77] The argument advanced by Lauristin,
that the proposed amendments did not sufficiently respect the rights of
the republics, was answered with the claim that 'only a strong union can
guarantee the effective development of all the republics'.[78] In the
words of one of the drafters of the amendments who attended this
meeting:

> The whole thing was very embarrassing. There were the Estonians, well
> prepared, making arguments on a high level of legal culture. No one on
> the subcommission even understood what they were saying. Only [Vice-
> President] Luk'yanov, who is trained as a lawyer, could talk with them.
> I think their [the Estonians'] ideas are not so bad. But the subcommission
> did not really consider them.[79]

Although this round of negotiations failed to resolve the matter,
Moscow was quick to signal its concern by dispatching Politburo
members V. M. Chebrikov, V. A. Medvedev and N. N. Slyun'kov to
Estonia, Latvia and Lithuania respectively to confer with top officials
in these republics and with representatives of their popular fronts.
These meetings achieved very little and may in some respects have been
counter-productive. Hours of Slyun'kov's discussions with political
officials and leaders of Sajudis, for instance, were carried live over
Lithuanian television. Lithuanians with whom I subsequently spoke
saw his performance as a heavy-handed attempt to steamroller his
opponents in debate. As one leader of Sajudis remembered:

> It was incredible. We were explaining patiently to him our objections to
> the Constitutional project and our own plans for the future direction of the
> Republic. He didn't understand. He just repeated the things he had said
> before or just ignored the points that we had brought up. He seemed able
> to see things only in one way. It was at times really quite embarrassing.[80]

In the wake of Medvedev's visit to Latvia, the Latvian Popular Front
took a formal position on the proposed Constitutional amendments that
characterized them as 'open counter-revolution'.[81] Immediately after
the departure of Chebrikov from Estonia, the Estonian Supreme Soviet

was called into special session to open a third front of resistance to the project.

On 16 November, the Estonian Supreme Soviet adopted a series of amendments to their Republic's Constitution that could nullify the effect of the entire legislative project. All economic resources in Estonia were declared the property of the Estonian people, with additional provision made for personal, private and mixed forms of property. Estonian law was proclaimed paramount on Estonian soil, and laws or acts of the national government would have effect in the Republic only after being registered by the Prezidium of the Estonian Supreme Soviet which reserved the right to suspend or modify them.[82] A Resolution passed unanimously at this same session reiterated the objections of the Estonians to the proposed amendments to the Constitution of the USSR and stipulated that any such Constitutional changes could only be considered valid if they were approved by all of the union republics.[83] These measures sought to reverse the previous pattern of federal relations in the USSR, whereby the centre granted certain rights and powers to the republics, with one in which the centre was itself constituted by grants of authority from sovereign union republics.

Moscow's immediate reply was rejection. The preparatory subcommission, with one dissenting vote and two abstentions, recommended to the Joint Commission on Legislative Proposals that the Estonian initiative be declared unconstitutional.[84] The latter, with its Latvian and Estonian deputies abstaining, made the same recommendation to the Prezidium of the Supreme Soviet[85] which, to no one's surprise, promptly complied.[86] However, the Estonian gambit, which spearheaded the broad opposition to the legislative project present in the three Baltic republics, impressed upon the central authorities the need to offer some concessions. As a result, they introduced some last-minute changes in the proposed amendments that represented the only substantial modifications in the project wrought by the nationwide assessment. First, each republic would be allowed to send eleven, rather than the originally proposed seven, of its deputies to the Council of Nationalities, thus increasing the number of representatives from the smaller union republics on the Supreme Soviet. Second, provision was made to ensure that each republic would be represented on the Council of the Union of the Supreme Soviet.[87] Third, while the central government would retain the authority to declare martial law or a state of emergency anywhere in the country, the final draft of the amendment to Article 119 required that it consult the prezidium of the supreme soviet of the republic in question before undertaking such measures.[88]

These concessions probably had some symbolic import. They did not, however, completely assuage opponents of the project in the Supreme Soviet itself. When the final vote was tallied, a handful of 'no' votes (5) and abstentions (27) served as reminders that opposition continued. Moreover, within a matter of days, the Estonian Supreme Soviet reconvened and defied Moscow again by reasserting what the central authorities had just declared unconstitutional, namely, the right of the republic to invalidate on its own soil the laws or acts of the all-union government.[89]

## CONCLUDING THOUGHTS ON THE ASSESSMENT AND DEBATE

Inasmuch as the legislative project, and the nationwide assessment and public debate that attended it, were processes mediating the transition of the Soviet Union toward a more effective governmental system within a more democratic political order, the ironies and inconsistencies noted in this chapter might be regarded as the more or less expected consequences of the new co-habitating with the old. Equally, they can be understood as manifestations of the contradiction contained in democratization from above. With respect to the project and the nationwide assessment, for instance, this was directly evident in the language of the Constitutional amendments and the discourse within which they were discussed. Much of the wording that appeared in the amendments departed from the sort of language that one ordinarily associates with constitutions. In addition to a description of the organizational structure of government and an enumeration of the powers assigned to its various bodies, the language of the amendments in question was interlarded with 'declarations and summonses [that] only superficially remind you of juridical acts'.[90] Article 130, for example, makes the Council of Ministers responsible to the Congress and the Supreme Soviet, the 'supreme organ of state power' and its 'continuously acting' sub-unit. Yet, as if unconvinced that the legislative organs would be able to exercise the power awarded them, Article 130 then requires the Council of Ministers to deliver an annual report to the Supreme Soviet, something that, presumably, any 'supreme organ' could demand itself. The

problem of tangled and inappropriate language was equally visible in
the nationwide assessment. As one journalist with legal training
remarked:

> I don't know whom the press expects to inform with the sorts of discus-
> sions that they publish. What do we see? Either glowing letters of
> approval from politically illiterate people or inaccessible commentaries
> from some professor or other that most readers find incomprehensible.[91]

But if the constraints inherent in the top-down process of Constitutional change and nationwide assessment enable us to understand some
of the anomalies that we have met, how might we characterize and
comprehend the public debate? Many of its participants regarded the
entire enterprise as an exercise in futility. 'This whole thing is happen-
ing because the Central Committee decided that it would occur,'
remarked one speaker at a public discussion. 'Not really,' replied a
member of the audience to the amusement of those assembled, 'it has
come from God!'[92] At another public meeting, a political activist from
the informal political club, Civic Dignity, railed against 'this fake
project, fake proposals and fake corrections.'[93] At a third, a representative from the Moscow Popular Front introduced the position
adopted by his organization on the project by remarking that it is useless
to criticize the project, for the authorities have already decided that it
will go forward without any real alterations.[94] His words were endorsed by several other speakers who commented:

- 'our government will not allow changes of substance in this
  project'.
- 'Gorbachev said before this all started that "we in the Politburo will
  soon be considering political reform". There you have it, *we* in the
  Politburo, not you!'
- 'spineless academics are the only voice that the Politburo will listen
  to!'
- 'the very fact that only one month is allowed for discussion of the
  project shows that the nationwide assessment is not serious.'

Yet not only were these individuals giving up their evenings to take part
in a process that they believed to be bogus from the start, but they
dutifully delivered their assessments to the authorities who, in their own
estimation, had no intention of paying them any heed.[95]

One final aspect of the public debate should not remain unmentioned. It was immensely alive. In contrast to dozens of meetings in the Soviet Union that I have sat through in the past where speakers addressed audiences preoccupied with private conversations or solitary reading, these discussions riveted the attention of all those present to the matter at hand. Often, speakers were unceremoniously interrupted by someone from the audience who could no longer contain his disagreement on some point that the speaker was making. Almost as soon as the first unscheduled interruption had occurred, other participants would leap to their feet to defend the initial speaker or to raise other issues that frequently had little or no relation to the topic under discussion. Order would be restored by a moderator who would remind one and all that 'comrades, we are not in the kitchen, we are trying to conduct an orderly discussion, and that means that we must follow procedures'. Chastened, those standing and, often, shouting from their places would meekly resume their seats. Within five or ten minutes, however, another such eruption would occur and the whole process would repeat itself.

The public debate, then, represented a celebration of democracy. Principles and ideals seemed urgently important. Details and facts, on the other hand, often went missing. The influence exercised by the image of American democracy was a case in point. During a long discussion of the project in the Law Faculty at Moscow State University for example, one professor, visibly annoyed by the arguments being presented, opined from her seat: 'I propose that we adopt the Constitution of the United States of America in full and be done with it'. The 100 or so people within earshot of this remark enthusiastically nodded their approval. At a discussion organized by the Group of Socialist Initiative, the moderator was entertaining remarks from the audience, point by point, on each of the draft amendments. On the topic of how the President of the Supreme Soviet was to be chosen, a member of the audience rose to his feet to endorse the idea of a national election for this office. 'We need a real President,' he said, 'one who is elected by all the people, just like in America.' The assent that this remark evoked was quickly dissipated, however, by another comment from the audience: 'In America, the people don't elect the President, the Senate does.' Somewhat uncertainly, the moderator seemed to take this statement as sufficient reason to end debate on that point.

The impression left by such exchanges was clear. Those in the public debate had a strong commitment to democracy; as individuals expressed their convictions in the company of their fellows, the commitment itself was reinforced many times over. America seemed to symbolize for those involved the democratic ideal. The 'real' America was, in a sense, beside the point. Within the discourse of the public debates, America represented that which the Soviet Union lacked. Freedom and democracy. A government of laws. The message delivered by the public debates to those in authority who might have been listening was also clear: We too shall have these things.

## NOTES

1.  V. G. Lomonosov's comments appeared in an interview published in *Pravda* (18 Nov. 1988).
2.  In a round-table discussion with other legal specialists that took place on the eve of the nationwide assessment, V. I. Kazimirchuk singled out this aspect of the standard process of public comment on draft legislation in the USSR to make his point that a genuine nationwide assessment of a legal project has never occurred there. His comments can be found in Yu. Feofanov, 'Vlast' i zakon', *Izvestiya* (16 Oct. 1988).
3.  R. F. Vasil'ev offered these observations at a meeting of the Law Faculty of Moscow State University on 27 October at which the legislative project was debated (hereafter cited as 'Law Faculty'). For similar comments, see I. Aleksandrov and E. Sukhov, 'Schastlivye sdelayut bol'she', *Sotsialisticheskaya industriya* (26 Oct. 1988).
4.  M. Kushtapin, 'Kommissiya odobrila popravki i predlozheniya', *Izvestiya* (20 Nov. 1988)
5.  A. Stepovoi, 'Prikazano srochno odobrit', *Izvestiya* (15 Nov. 1988).
6.  V. Lyubitskii, 'Zakony po kotorym nam zhit'', *Pravda* (21 Nov. 1988).
7.  'Podlinno narodnye zakony', *Izvestiya* (6 Dec. 1988).
8.  *Ibid.* See also M. S. Gorbachev's Report to the Supreme Soviet, 'K polnovlastiyu Sovetov i sozdaniyu sotsialisticheskogo pravovogo gosudarstva', *Izvestiya* (30 Nov. 1988).
9.  *Predlozheniya i Zamechaniya po proektu zakona SSSR ob izmeneniyakh i dopolneniyakh Konstitutsii SSSR (Po materialam Prezidiumov Verkhovnykh Sovetov soyuznykh respublik, ministerstv, vedomstv, gazet i pisem grazhdan)* (mimeo; Prezidium of Supreme Soviet, USSR: Moscow, 3 Nov. 1988).
10. Legal specialists to whom these synopses were sent expressed their 'surprise' to me during interviews that these items, which they had expected to draw the most public criticism, were not surfacing in the nationwide assessment.
11. *Predlozheniya i Zamechaniya po proektu zakona SSSR ob izmeneniyakh i dopolneniyakh Konstitutsii SSSR, ne voshedshie v predydushchie vypuski (Po materialam Prezidiumov Verkhovnykh Sovetov soyuznykh respublik, ministerstv, vedomstv, gazet i pisem grazhdan,* Vypusk 4, Chast' I, Glavy 12, 13, and Vypusk 4, Chast' II, Glava 15 i dr. stati (mimeo; Prezidium of Supreme Soviet, USSR: Moscow, 15 Nov. 1988).

12. *Sravnitel'naya Tablitsa proekta Zakona SSSR ob izmeneniyakh i dopolneniyakh Konstitutsii (Osnovogo Zakona) SSSR, opublikovannogo dlya vsenarodnogo obsuzheniya, i predlagaemykh popravok teksta proekta* (mimeo; Prezidium of Supreme Soviet, USSR: Moscow, 15 Nov. 1988).

13. The one modification of import that did not appear in this document concerned the number of representatives that each republic would send to the Supreme Soviet's Council of Nationalities (see below).

14. M. Kushtapin, 'Vsenarodnaya ekspertiza', *Izvestiya* (11 Nov. 1988).

15. Interview (16 Nov. 1988).

16. See his interview with V. Khatyntsev, 'Zakonotvorchestvo', *Pravda* (7 Nov. 1988).

17. Another such case involved the election of judges at the district and regional levels. The working group that prepared the draft of the Constitutional amendments preferred the arrangement adopted at the Nineteenth Party Conference whereby judges at these levels would be elected by soviets at higher levels. In their initial draft, however, they included a different provision which called for the election of such judges by soviets at the corresponding level. After suitable public criticism of the initial draft, the provision was changed to what had been originally intended by the preparatory subcommission at its session of 18 November. See M. Kushtapin, 'Kommissiya odobrila popravki i predlozheniya', *Izvestiya* (19 Nov. 1988).

18. Gorbachev, 'K polnovlastiyu Sovetov...'.

19. V. Shchepotkin, 'Grazhdane pravyat Konstitutsiyu', *Izvestiya* (2 Nov. 1988).

20. I. Karpenko, 'Zakony, po kotorym zhit' i rabotat', *Izvestiya* (26 Nov. 1988).

21. For a detailed account of much of the commentary that we are not here considering, see Stephen White, '"Democratization" in the USSR' (mimeo; Glasgow: Glasgow University, 1989).

22. 'Razvivaya narodovlastie', *Pravda* (13 Nov. 1988); T. Volkov, 'Sporyat pis'ma mezh soboyu', *ibid.* (16 Nov. 1988); Al'bert Plutnik, 'Vse v nashei vlasti, kogda vlast'—nasha', *Izvestiya* (9 Nov. 1988).

23. *Pravda* (14 Nov. 1988).

24. Gurili's comments were made at a meeting in the experimental, self-governing micro-raion, Brateevo, located in southwest Moscow, on 18 November 1988 (subsequent references to this meeting are rendered 'Brateevo Meeting'). During a public meeting called by the Club for the Assessment of the Constitution on 3 November 1988, comments similar to Gurili's were made by two speakers (subsequent references to this meeting are rendered 'Constitutional Club').

25. 'Brateevo Meeting'. This speaker answered her own question with the statement: 'Certainly not what the press says about them'.

26. *Pravda* (26 Oct. 1988). A similar argument with a slightly different point can be found in L. Kudryashov's letter, published in *Argumenty i fakty*, No. 45 (5-11 Nov. 1988).

27. I heard comments to this effect at most of the eleven public discussions on the legislative project that I attended in Moscow during the period of nationwide assessment. My notes from one of these, sponsored by the Moscow Club for the Assessment of the Constitution which drew over 400 participants on the night of 3 November, contain references to each of these criticisms. ('Constitutional Club').

    For an example of a published statement maintaining that the draft proposals depart from the principles approved at the Nineteenth Party Congress, see 'Vlast' Sovetov, vlast' naroda', *Pravda* (31 Oct. 1988).

28.  These points were made in the course of interviews with two Soviet journalists, an official in Moscow's city government, three Soviet legal specialists who did not participate in drafting the project and two who did.

29.  Authors of the draft legislation made these points during interviews on a few occasions. Two of the authors also made them at a meeting called by the Political Club of the graduate students of the Law Faculty of Moscow State University (hereafter cited as 'Graduate Student Political Club').

30.  See V. Kopeikin's letter in *Argumenty i fakty*, No. 45 (5-11 Nov. 1988).

31.  This point was made by two graduate students during the discussion at 'Law Faculty'. It also appeared in V. Popov's remarks that were published under the title 'Vlast' Sovetov, vlast' naroda', *Pravda* (31 Oct. 1988).

32.  'Constitutional Club'.

33.  'Brateevo meeting'. One of the few participants in the nationwide assessment who made this same criticism was Boris Kurashvili. 'How [is it possible] to prevent such deputies from becoming elected by their cronies in the governing apparatus of a specific organization?' he asked his interlocutor, Andrei Romanov, in an interview published in *Moskovskie novosti*, No. 47 (20 Nov. 1988).

34.  Members of Leningrad Perestroika, A. N. Alekseev, G. A. Bogomolov and Yu. M. Nesterov complained that the provision whereby public organizations appoint one-third of the deputies is simply a method to include in the legislature those big shots who could never survive a popular election. 'Shag vpered—dva shaga nazad', *Arkhiv khronografa* (mimeo; Leningrad, 28 Oct. 1988), p. 2.

     Similar arguments can be found in the commentary of the Moscow-based informal political group, Grazhdanskoe dostoinstvo, 'Ob izmeneniyakh i dopolneniyakh Konstitutsii (Osnovogo zakona) SSSR' (mimeo; Moscow, Nov., 1988).

35.  Writing on behalf of the Court, its First Deputy President, S. I. Gusev, observed that 'it would be more democratic if elections were directly from the population'.

36.  All of the excerpted press comment on this issue took this form in *Predlozheniya i Zamechaniya po proektu …* (3 Nov. 1988). For an example of how the press tended to trivialize this problem, see V. Trushkov, 'Chistyi svet narodovlastiya', *Moskovskaya pravda* (19 Nov. 1988).

37.  M. Chulaki, 'Skol'ko golosov v odnikh rukakh', *Izvestiya* (4 Nov. 1988).

38.  G. Barabashev, 'Prostaya demokratiya eshche ne znachit nadezhnaya', *Izvestiya* (4 Nov. 1988).

39.  Barabashev made these remarks during an interview (8 May 1989) and went on to note that he had produced a modification for the final draft of the project that was endorsed by the Joint Commission on Legislative Proposals which clearly distinguished between these two principles of representation. In the rush of events, however, this modification was somehow left out of the final version. Another member of the working group that drafted the Constitutional amendments, V. Vasil'ev, claimed in an article published after the project had been ratified that the Soviet Constitution now contained two principles of representation, one 'territorial' and the other 'corporative'. See his 'Realizm i novatorstvo', *Sovety narodnykh deputatov*, (Feb., 1989), pp. 14-22; esp., pp. 14-15.

40.  *Inter alia*, B. Strashun, '… net, po odnomu spisku', *Izvestiya* (23 Nov. 1988); M. Kushtapin's interview with V. E. Guliev, *ibid.* (19 Nov. 1988).

41. This introduction enjoyed considerable popularity at a meeting of the Group of Socialist Initiative (24 Oct. 1988) at which the draft legislation was discussed (hereafter, 'Group of Socialist Initiative').
42. 'Law Faculty'.
43. 'Constitutional Club'.
44. See, in particular, the letters from two law professors, V. Vengerov and M. Piskotin, published in *Izvestiya* (22 Nov. 1988).
45. Numerous speakers made this point, always with the accompaniment of considerable applause, at 'Brateevo Meeting', 'Constitutional Club' and 'Graduate Student Political Club'.
46. 'Constitutional Club'.
47. 'Constitutional Club'.
48. B. Kurashvili, 'Verkhovnaya vlast': iz proshlogo v budushchee', *Izvestiya* (15 Nov. 1988).
49. 'Law Faculty'.
50. Grazhdanskoe dostoinstvo, 'Ob izmeneniyakh i dopolneniyakh ...'.
51. See, for example, the interview given by I. N. Kuznetsov to V. Saklakov that appeared in *Sovetskaya Rossiya* (25 Oct. 1988); B. Lazarev, 'Dostionstva novatsii besspomy', *Izvestiya* (15 Nov. 1988).
52. 'Graduate Student Political Club'.
53. V. Volynskii noted this in 'Vlast' Sovetov, vlast' naroda', *Pravda* (31 Oct. 1988).
54. Kurashvili in *Moskovskie novosti;* D. Bakatin and I. Popov, 'Garantii pravovogo gosudarstva', *Izvestiya* (25 Nov. 1988). See also the letters to the Editor of *Izvestiya* by V. Yan'kov (4 Nov. 1988), E. Nagaev (19 Nov. 1988), and I. Kondrat'ev (25 Nov. 1988).
55. Chulaki, 'Skol'ko golosov ...'. The same point was made with more acrimony at 'Brateevo Meeting', and by Alekseev, Bogomolov and Nesterov, 'Shag vpered—dva shaga nazad', pp. 2-5.
56. Kurashvili in *Moskovskie novosti.*
57. 'Constitutional Club'.
58. Chulaki, 'Skol'ko golosov ...'.
59. B. Gabrichidze, 'Chto sdelaet Sovety sil'nee', *Izvestiya* (27 Oct. 1988).
60. Grazhdanskoe dostoinstvo, 'Ob izmeneniyakh i dopolneniyakh ...'. Interestingly, Kurashvili, who had propagated the notion of combining the offices of party and government leaders before the decision to do so was taken at the Nineteenth Party Conference, came out against the idea of President of the Supreme Soviet as it appeared in the draft amendments because, without a multi-party system, he felt that too much power would be concentrated in a single pair of hands. See his 'Verkhovnaya vlast' ...'.
61. 'Brateevo Meeting'.
62. 'Group of Socialist Initiative'.
63. 'Constitutional Club'.
64. 'Constitutional Club'; 'Brateevo Meeting'.
65. V. Savitskii, 'Tak kakoi sud nam nuzhen?' *Pravda* (26 Oct. 1988); E. Smolentsev, 'Garantirovat' sudu nezavisimost'', *Izvestiya* (18 Nov. 1988); letters from G. Gubin and V. Pisarchuk, *ibid.* (2 Nov. 1988). This issue was also addressed in some of the public debates that I attended. One, that took place on 25 October in the Department of State Law and Soviet Construction at Moscow State University, reached immediate consensus on the question: return to the resolution adopted at the Party Conference. At another, however, Professor A. A. Mishin went further by offering the opinion, seconded by others, that in order to establish an independent judiciary in place of 'party courts', judges should be popularly elected and serve for life. 'Law Faculty'.

66. 'Brateevo meeting'; 'Group of Socialist Initiative'.
67. For an exchange of views on this issue, see the letters published in *Izvestiya* (13 Nov. 1988).
68. See my '"Informals" and Popular Fronts', *Detente*, No. 14 (1989), pp. 3-8, 27.
69. *Inter alia*, the interview given by Oleg Lugus, 'Regional'nyi khozraschet: svershitsya li chudo?', *Sovetskaya Estoniya* (20 Oct. 1988); the interview given by V. Mal'kovskii, 'Khozraschet goroda', *ibid.* (19 Oct. 1988); B. Saul, 'Khozraschet territorii', *Izvestiya* (10 Sept. 1988); *Proekty obshchei programmy i ustava Litovskogo dvizheniya za perestroiku* (Vilnius: Tsk KP Litvy, 1988).
70. *Inter alia*, the interview given by Indrek Toome, 'Vse khotyat peremen', *Novoe vremya*, No. 39 (1988), pp. 21-23; the account of a discussion among factory workers published under the title 'Slozhnye voprosy—neodnoznachnye otvety', *Sovetskaya Latviya* (5 Oct. 1988).
71. For early examples, see the speeches of R. I. Songaila and V. I. Valjas, first secretaries of the Lithuanian and Estonian parties, respectively, to the Nineteenth Party Conference, *Izvestiya* (2 July 1988). See also the speeches of A. K. Zitmanis, deputy from Latvia, and I. K. Kubilyus, deputy from Lithuania, to a session of the Supreme Soviet, *Izvestiya* (29 Oct. 1988). Dozens of deputies from the Baltic set a precedent at this session by voting against the measures recommended by the Supreme Soviet's Prezidium. See Jonathan Steele, 'Soviet deputies break tradition by voting against', *Manchester Guardian Weekly* (6 Nov. 1988).
72. Interview (28 Nov. 1988).
73. See, for example, the interview given by Tiit Kyabin, 'Vlast' Sovetov, vlast' naroda', *Pravda* (30 Oct. 1988); letter from K. Valanchyus, *Izvestiya* (19 Nov. 1988).
74. Interview with Virgilius Chepaitis, Executive Secretary of Sajudis (30 Nov. 1988).
75. This point was made by representatives from each of the popular fronts in the Baltic who addressed a gathering of some 500 students and faculty at Moscow State University on 4 November 1988.
76. Interview with Chepaitis.
77. M. Kushtapin, 'Vsenarodnaya ekspertiza', *Izvestiya* (11 Nov. 1988).
78. V. Khatuntsev, 'Obratnaya svyaz', *Pravda* (31 Nov. 1988).
79. Interview (12 Nov. 1988).
80. Interview with Chepaitis.
81. *Sovetskaya Latviya* (19 Nov. 1988).
82. *Sovetskaya Estoniya* (19 Nov. 1988).
83. 'O predlozheniyakh po proektam Zakona SSSR ob izmeneniyakh i dopolneniyakh Konstitutsii (Osnovnogo Zakona) SSSR i Zakona SSSR o vyborakh narodnykh deputatov SSSR', Postanovlenie Verkovnogo Soveta Estonskoi Sovetskoi Sotsialisticheskoi Respubliki (17 Nov. 1988). For an outline of the actions undertaken jointly by the Communist Party and Popular Front in Estonia in this respect, see the unsigned article 'Proshlogodnii opyt—na sluzhbu dnyu segodnyashnemu', *Kommunist Estonii*, No. 1 (1989), pp. 13-19.
84. V. Lyubitskii, 'Zakony po kotorym nam zhit''.
85. M. Kushtapin, 'Deputaty golosuyut za popravki', *Izvestiya* (20 Nov. 1988).
86. *Izvestiya* (28 Nov. 1988).
87. See the report delivered by G. P. Razumovskii, Chairperson of the Supreme Soviet's Joint Commission of Legislative Proposals, to the session of the Supreme Soviet at which the legislative project was formally ratified, *Izvestiya* (2 Dec. 1988). The combined effect of these two provisions increased the size of the Supreme Soviet from an initially projected membership of 442 to 542.

88. A somewhat stronger version of this provision had been introduced into the deliberations of this session of the Supreme Soviet on the previous day by the Georgian leader, D. I. Patiashvili. Such a proposal had also been placed before the previous session by P. P. Goryunov, deputy from Estonia. *Izvestiya* (31 Oct. 1988).

89. *Sovetskaya Estoniya* (10 Dec. 1988).

90. V. Prozorov made this comment in an interview given to Yu. Feofanov, 'Ot proekta do zakona', *Izvestiya* (9 Dec. 1988).

91. Interview with Oleg Shcherbakov (26 Nov. 1988).

92. 'Brateevo Meeting'.

93. 'Graduate Student Political Club'.

94. 'Constitutional Club'.

95. Shortly before the end of the period of nationwide assessment, Moscow's Popular Front sent a telegram to the Supreme Soviet's Joint Commission on Legislative Proposals outlining the group's objections to the legislative project, the method by which the changes were scheduled to be adopted and the shortness of the term of popular discussion. The Club for the Assessment of the Constitution, which sponsored the meeting at which these remarks were made, did the same.

# 5. NATIONAL ELECTIONS

The period of nationwide assessment brought the wings of Gorbachev's reform coalition into open opposition. During the electoral campaigns that ensued, this opposition spilled over into the streets. As Soviet commentators have remarked, the political clashes that occurred were the more or less predictable outcome of the dynamic contradiction that drove the reform process. The Constitutional amendments and new Law on Elections opened up, on the one hand, an opportunity for the population to organize and to influence via public elections the composition of the government. On the other hand, this legislation also enabled the apparatus to intervene at various stages in the process in order to limit that same opportunity.[1] Struggle in a number of forms—subterfuge, manipulation, public demonstration, intimidation, violence and, ultimately, voting—became the means by which contests between democratic and conservative forces were settled during the electoral phase of the democratization process.[2]

In part, the intensity and scope of the electoral struggle derived from the legislative project that set it in motion. The apparatus, for instance, regularly attempted to utilize the 'filters' emplaced in the procedures for nominating candidates in order to keep their opponents off balance and, more importantly, off the ballot. Democratic forces, in turn, often met these attempts with the only resources available to them: publicity, legal appeals and the weight of their (mobilized) numbers. Sometimes they succeeded in clearing away the impediments thrown up by the apparatus and went on to score some impressive victories at the polls. However, the sites and outcomes of the clashes that occurred between these opposing forces were also shaped and influenced by another factor, viz., the very machinery that had been set up to organize and conduct the elections.

The immediate encounters that took place between the apparatus and the forces oriented toward democracy were mediated by electoral commissions in each electoral district and within each public organization entitled to name deputies to the Congress. The enforcement of election procedures fell to these commissions, but since they themselves were ordinarily controlled by the apparatus, their role as impartial referee was severely compromised and they often became party to the very conflicts that they were formally charged to regulate. We therefore defer for the moment the question of how the electoral commissions actively shaped the corpus of candidates and the contours of electoral competition in order to situate these commissions within the overall structure of the electoral machinery, turning our attention first to that structure itself.

## THE ORGANIZATIONAL STRUCTURE OF THE ELECTORAL PROCESS

Before completing the work of its Twelfth Extraordinary Session, the Supreme Soviet initiated the first stage of the electoral process by naming a 35-member Central Electoral Commission (CEC). According to its Chairperson, V. P. Orlov, 'representatives of all the union republics [and] of many labour collectives [and] public organizations' were included in its membership.[3] What Orlov neglected to mention, however, was the fact that the selection process by which these 'representatives' were chosen was thoroughly controlled by top party officials and by the apparatus within the trade unions that formally made nominations to the Supreme Soviet.[4] Moreover, the work of the CEC was supervised by Vice-President Luk'yanov who attended all save one of its meetings and acted as 'a political guide for the Commission'.[5] At its first session on 6 December, the CEC approved the boundaries of the 1,500 districts in which public elections were to be held and submitted estimates to the government for the campaign and administrative costs (ultimately fixed at 156,470,000 roubles[6]) of the elections.[7] Thereafter, it met frequently and discharged four general functions.

First, the CEC registered and monitored the activities of the electoral commissions formed in the localities and in those public organizations with the right to name deputies. The role of the CEC in this respect was ambiguous. Its Chairperson defined it as uniformly enforcing the letter of the law.[8] But its Secretary, who expressed doubts about the ability of the citizenry to make informed choices as to who should represent them, saw the CEC's role as one of assisting local electoral commissions in deciding not only how many but which particular candidates to register in their districts.[9] Moreover, since the CEC set a very early date (15 December)[10] for completion of the process of selecting members to the local electoral commissions, it all but ensured that the composition of each was determined by the apparatus. In this respect, the new elections much resembled the old. Local party officials simply drafted individuals into service on the electoral commissions, regularly failing to notify labour collectives of their right to nominate representatives to the commissions[11] or conveniently ignoring legitimate nominations when such had been put forth.[12] Thereafter, the local apparatus often withheld vital information from these commissions while making the real decisions themselves behind a façade of public involvement.[13] As one local party official explained to a newspaper reporter: 'Nobody has taken from us the responsibility of conducting the elections'.[14]

Second, the CEC interpolated the legal provisions governing their work and, in the process, took some important decisions bearing on the outcome of the elections. One of these assisted opponents of the apparatus by enabling all registered candidates to select a campaign staff of ten persons who were paid out of the election funds disbursed by the CEC. Another decision, however, proved to be of enormous advantage to the apparatus. It stipulated that should a given electoral commission choose to call a pre-electoral district meeting, then (a) at least half of the delegates must be drawn from organizations in the district that had not nominated a candidate, (b) the local electoral commission would decide which of these organizations could send delegates to this meeting, and (c) all delegations attending this meeting would be equal in number. These provisions enabled electoral commissions to choose those labour collectives in which delegate selection could be controlled by the apparatus and thus to pack pre-electoral district meetings with reliable people. This was often accomplished by excluding from participation labour collectives in large enterprises and by awarding disproportionate influence to small groups (such as schools). The apparatus, already in control of the commissions, could thereby dominate the pre-electoral district meetings as well, and through these intermediaries determine, as it had in the past, who would stand for election.

Third, in accordance with statute and in consultation with the top officials of public organizations, the CEC made a number of determinations with respect to which of the public organizations would be eligible to select deputies to the Congress and the number of seats allotted to each. A few disputes broke out on these points as certain organizations that appeared to meet the legal requirements of selecting deputies were denied the right to do so. In the end, the CEC rejected the claims of the Association of Cooperatives and the Inter-Regional Federation of Cooperatives on this score,[15] but reached a compromise with the Movement of Volunteers for the Conservation of Nature by arranging for it to name two deputies on the list of 75 that had been apportioned to the Komsomol.[16]

Finally, the CEC intervened on numerous occasions into the electoral process, both in response to complaints and by way of spot-checking procedures. In a number of instances discussed below, these interventions rescued democratic candidates whose legal rights had been violated by opponents in the apparatus. In this respect, the CEC often played an important role in upholding the law and in guaranteeing a modicum of fairness in the electoral process. Indeed, the electoral success of many democratic candidates would have been impossible to achieve without its help. Yet in many instances it is difficult to determine whether the CEC was indeed thwarting the designs of ill-intentioned groups of local bosses or simply instructing local election officials on just what procedures to follow in a given case, so great were the confusion and uncertainty obtaining in the novel circumstances of a competitive election.[17]

This same confusion and uncertainty also affected the CEC itself.[18] In perhaps the most egregious example of this situation, the newspaper, *Izvestiya*, having wearied of receiving phone calls and letters from readers wanting this or that aspect of the election procedures explained and clarified, published an interview with E. Koveshnikov, head of the CEC's juridical staff. The newspaper made a point of saying: Don't call us, call them, 'the most authoritative and qualified' people around.[19] Koveshnikov took the opportunity to respond to a few common queries from readers and, in so doing, confidently claimed that candidates were at liberty to solicit campaign contributions from organizations and private individuals. As the newspaper pointed out some days later, this was an unfortunate error on Koveshnikov's part for his advice actually contravened clear stipulations in the Law on Elections regarding equal funding for all candidates.[20] Stranger still, the matter of private financing had been discussed by the CEC's juridical staff the very day before Koveshnikov gave his interview, and he himself was party to the decision that disallowed any private funding.[21]

## NOMINATIONS AND ELECTIONS IN THE PUBLIC ORGANIZATIONS

A total of 39 public organizations named deputies to the Congress. The number of seats awarded to each ranged from 100 (the Communist Party and the All-Union Council of Trade Unions) to just one (e.g., the All-Union Volunteer Society for the Struggle for Sobriety, the All-Union Society of Philatelists). By the close of the nominations phase, a total of 880 candidates had been registered by public organizations for the 750 seats earmarked for them in the Congress.[22] In some instances, the nominations process within public organizations was genuinely competitive and generated no small amount of excitement. In most, however, it was thoroughly orchestrated by the executive apparatus of the respective organizations, leading one reporter to note that it is far from the case 'that the strictures corresponding to the spirit and even the letter of the Law on Elections have been everywhere observed'.[23]

The Communist Party began the selection of its 100 deputies with a summons from its Electoral Commission that called on party members to submit the names of prospective candidates to their respective primary party organizations, whence they would be sent up the organizational ladder, with the possibility of deletions and additions occurring on each rung.[24] Accordingly, the 31,500 candidates proposed by primary party organizations were reduced to 3,500 by party committees at the next level. This number was further whittled to 207 by republic and regional party bodies, reinflated to 312 by the Central Committee and finally fixed at 100 by the Politburo.[25] It would seem fair to conclude, therefore, that the election of deputies (the same 100 'nominated' by the Politburo) that took place on 15 March at the Plenum of the Central Committee (enlarged to 641 members) represented no more than a parody of democracy. Although millions of party members had participated at one stage or another in the process, it was in the Politburo that the actual 'election' occurred. Moreover, as Boris Nikol'skii, the Editor of *Neva*, subsequently pointed out, by nominating

100 candidates to fill its allotted 100 seats in the Congress, the Communist Party leadership in fact sent an important signal to lower party bodies that competition in the upcoming elections could, and perhaps should, be avoided.[26]

However, certain aspects of the selection process were, if not democratic, at least quite novel. First, deputies chosen by the Communist Party included only some 23 individuals employed in the apparatus. The majority was composed of lower-level administrators in industry and agriculture (factory directors, brigade leaders, collective farm chairpersons and so forth) and leaders in the fields of science and culture. In a sense, then, the Politburo was saying to those at middle levels of its apparatus: If you want to become a deputy, you will have to stand for public election yourself. As we see below, many in the apparatus chose to do so, often with disastrous results.

Second, at the enlarged Plenum that approved the Politburo's list, V. A. Koptyurg, Chairperson of the party's Electoral Commission, made mention of the fact that a number of letters from rank-and-file party members had reached his office that contained decidedly negative evaluations of many of the party's better-known newly-named deputies.[27] He then proceeded to name the individuals in question: nine members of the Politburo, including the General Secretary himself, and another two dozen or so luminaries, among them the Editor of *Pravda* and the President of the Soviet Academy of Sciences. With respect to the Politburo members, Koptyurg summarized the nature of the criticisms in question and cited in some cases the number of negative letters received: Gorbachev (3), Zaikov (9), Yakovlev (2) and, finishing first in this category, Ligachev with 25.

Third, the party's Electoral Commission published the results of the final voting. Although no candidate came close to suffering defeat, the tallies were not without interest. They showed that the larger shares of the negative votes had been reserved for the more prominent nominees, especially for members of the Politburo and particularly for Ligachev, the reputed leader of the conservative faction who again outdistanced the others by capturing 78 'no' votes.[28]

Among the other public organizations entitled to send sizable blocs of their members to the Congress, the process of nominating and electing deputies transpired much as it did in the Communist Party. While over 1,000 nominations were sent up from the ranks to the All-Union Council of Trade Unions, only three of these names appeared on the final list of nominees adopted by an enlarged Plenum of the Central Committee of the Trade Unions.[29] The 100 deputies elected at the subsequent plenary session were drawn from a list of 114 nominees.[30] In the Komsomol only 207 nominations were introduced from below. The Komsomol's Central Committee reduced this number to 102 and later, at an enlarged Plenum, elected its 75 deputies.[31] The Committee of Soviet Women together with the national association of women's councils convened to nominate their candidates in joint session and reduced some 200 nominations proposed from the ranks to a list of 81, of which 79 were selected by the joint prezidium and two were put forward from the floor. The latter two were chosen for purposes of 'geographic' representation. As one of the nominators remarked: 'Comrades, how can we offend Belorussia? I go there often. It is such a republic, such a republic! They are able to feed and shoe themselves!'[32] This same notion of geography later influenced the final selection of 75 deputies from among the 81 candidates.[33] So, too, did the organizational rank of the contenders inasmuch as those successful candidates who drew the largest numbers of negative votes tended to be those who occupied prominent positions in the government and in public organizations.[34]

In a number of instances, the central organs of public organizations seem to have appropriated to themselves the sole right to name deputies. It took only half an hour for the Council of Collective Farms to approve a list of 58 candidates (a figure equal to its allotted number of seats) that had been prepared for it by officials in the State Agro-Industrial Committee.[35] Again, although over 100 candidates had been proposed from below to the Central Council of the All-Union Society of Inventors, its Electoral Commission chose to register only five of them, the exact number of deputies awarded to it.[36] A joint meeting of the Union of Soviet Societies for Friendship and Cultural Ties with Foreign Countries and the association, Rodina, likewise produced five candidates for the five posts to which they were entitled.[37] Subsequently, all five were elected deputies.[38] Within the Union of Journalists, progressive candidates, such as E. V. Yakovlev and V. A. Korotich fell victim to rather arbitrary rulings handed down by that organization's executive body,[39] while those supervising the elections in the Soviet Committee in Defence of Peace turned a blind eye to violations of the Law on Elections that injured, fatally it seemed, the candidacy of Georgii Arbatov.[40]

In other cases, however, more democratic practices prevailed. The nominations meeting at a Plenum of the Union of Cinematographers got off to a dreary bureaucratic start with a prepared list of nominees read out from the Prezidium and little apparent interest displayed by the audience. As the proceedings progressed, however, the tone of the discussion sharpened and soon the meeting became a rather stormy one that continued for two days, almost around the clock. In the end, 20 candidates, almost all of whom had been nominated from the floor, were registered to compete for the Union's ten seats in the Congress.[41] Similar contests occurred in the Writers' Union[42] and in the lecturers' association, Znanie.[43] The largest and longest display of political fireworks, however, found a somewhat unlikely venue in one of the country's more staid and decorous institutions, the Academy of Sciences.

At its first meeting on 26 December, the Prezidium of the Academy decided to broaden the representation of the scientific community in the new legislature by giving five of its 30 seats in the Congress of People's Deputies to the newly-formed Union of Scientific Societies and Associations.[44] It then convened in a enlarged plenary session on 18 January to register its own candidates for the remaining 25 seats. Those attending this meeting, however, rejected 98 of the 121 proposed nominees, leaving the Academy two candidates short of its quota in the Congress. A decision to open nominations from the floor was taken and then reversed when V. N. Kudryavtsev, the Academy's Vice-President, mounted the rostrum and persuaded the hall to close nominations and solve the problem of a deficit of candidates by ceding five more of its seats to the Union of Scientific Societies and Associations.[45]

A number of contextual factors appear to have contributed to the storm of protest that this meeting subsequently provoked. While formally not undemocratic, the voting at the Academy's enlarged Plenum displayed to many small concern for the wishes of the general membership since precisely those who had been nominated by the largest number of the Academy's constituent institutes were knocked out of contention at this meeting.[46] Moreover, the list of these popular but unsuccessful candidates read like an abbreviated roster of the nation's leading progressive figures: Andrei Sakharov, Roald Sagdeev, Tatyana Zaslavskaya, Gavriil Popov, Dmitrii Likhachev and others. Since it was an open secret that these same individuals had long been conducting a struggle within the Academy against its senior and thoroughly conser-

vative officials, it seemed blatantly obvious to many that the conservatives were avenging themselves for the past by attempting to deny the
progressives a political future.[47] Finally, the donation of yet another
five seats to the Union of Scientific Societies and Associations ensured
that individuals such as Sakharov, who was not a member of any of the
28 groups housed under that Union's umbrella, would have no chance
to stand as candidates before their peers in the academic community.[48]

Incensed by this turn of events, members of the Academy and others
began bombarding the Academy's Prezidium, the CEC and the press
with angry letters and telegrams.[49] The CEC reviewed the case and
upheld the actions of the Academy's Prezidium and Electoral Commission, arguing, unconvincingly as things turned out, that those reform
leaders who had been denied registration by the Academy still had time
to find a place on the ballot in some electoral district.[50] This decision
precipitated a boisterous protest staged on the steps of the Academy a
few day later by over 1,000 supporters of the excluded democrats.[51]

Jolted by the realization that a revolt was brewing in the ranks of the
Academy, the authorities began scrambling for a compromise solution.
A series of meetings followed that involved, at various times, the CEC,
officers of the Academy and its Electoral Commission, the directors and
party secretaries of academic institutes as well as leaders of a newly-
organized inter-institutional initiative group, For Democratic Elections
in the Academy of Sciences.[52] In the end, a compromise was arrived
at by supplementing the 903 voters in the Academy with another 554
delegates chosen by academic institutions around the country who were
expected to reflect a more progressive orientation in the scientific
community. The three-day meeting convened in mid-March provided
a forum for impassioned speeches and denunciations of the Academy's
old guard, said to be oblivious to the democratic transformation sweeping the country and woefully and out of step with the requirements of
the time. To make the point clearly, the meeting passed a vote of
no-confidence in the Academy's Electoral Commission[53] and then
proceeded to reject all but eight of the 23 nominees before it.[54] The
new election prompted by these actions took place the following month
and witnessed victories for many of the reform leaders who had earlier
been excluded, among them Andrei Sakharov, Roald Sagdeev, Dmitrii
Likhachev and Nikolai Shmelev.[55]

## NOMINATIONS IN THE ELECTORAL DISTRICTS

Although the new Law on Elections provided for the nomination of an 'unlimited number of candidates' to compete in elections to the Congress, the mechanisms that it established for proposing and registering them became the grounds on which innumerable battles were fought on the issue of just who the candidates would be. In general, prospective candidates had to cross one and, often, two thresholds. The first involved obtaining a majority of votes from one of the nominating bodies—labour collectives or meetings of voters in their places of residence with at least 500 in attendance.[56] The second concerned the pre-electoral district meetings that were called by local electoral commissions in 868 of the country's 1,500 constituencies[57] in order to winnow the number of nominees who had crossed the first threshold. We begin our discussion, then, with what occurred during the first stage of the nominations process.

*Initial Nominations.* During the pre-registration phase of the nominations process (26 December - 24 January), some 7,558 potential candidates were put forward. This yielded a nationwide average of just over five candidates per seat, varying from 190 constituencies in which only one individual had been nominated to one constituency in which 30 potential candidates had been named.[58]

For some, the path to nomination seems to have been relatively easy. For instance, in Kazakhstan, each of the Republic's 17 obkom first secretaries was nominated to stand for office in a constituency in which his name alone would appear on the ballot.[59] In Moscow's self-administering community, Brateevo, a lively meeting with over 1,000 residents in attendance debated the merits of two individuals who had been proposed by the community's coordinating committee. It was well past midnight when a vote confirmed the nomination of one of them.[60] In most cases, however, citizens' initiatives appeared to encounter resistance from the local authorities.

One method by which local elites attempted to shut out challenges to their preferred candidates during the initial stage of the nominations process involved the manipulation of the nominating meetings that were held in labour collectives. One ally in this endeavour was the force of inertia, owing to the fact that local elites had always nominated the candidates of their choice behind the façade of unanimous affirmations from (de-politicized) workers. The passivity induced by this longstanding practice meant that many simply acquiesced in continuing the old ways under the new circumstances.[61] However, when this inertia was overcome by groups of politically active workers, local elites often manipulated the nominations procedures and machinery to ward off unwelcome challengers.

One variation on this approach that applied especially to nominations in the large enterprises witnessed the local apparatus controlling communications in such a way that only their candidates became known to many of the shop-level delegates who attended the selection conferences.[62] Although this tactic did not reflect well on the apparatus' attitude toward democracy and fair play, it was perfectly legal. Other stratagems employed by local elites, however, straddled and often crossed the boundaries of the legal framework. According to some reports, local party committees in certain areas issued directives to functionaries at the factory level to carry out a 'struggle' against informal democratically-oriented groups seeking to nominate their own candidates.[63] Accustomed to regard such directives as the law incarnate, the apparatus in many places simply took it upon themselves to mow down would-be challenges as they saw fit. The tactics employed by the apparatus in this struggle varied from place to place. In some instances, the example of local notables declining nomination in deference to an even larger luminary was meant—along with a warning: 'Don't you know whom you're going up against?'—to dissuade challengers from pursuing their own nominations.[64] In other cases, procedural manipulations,[65] orchestrated efforts to smear those whom informal political groups were attempting to nominate,[66] threats to one's career[67] and, indeed, to one's physical safety[68] were relied upon to discourage candidates and their supporters from bucking the powers that be.

In a few instances, however, determined individuals managed to crack the icy resistance of officialdom. N. Belous of Tomsk received a summons to the city headquarters of the party in the wake of his nomination by a labour collective. When pressure applied by the party committee failed to persuade him to withdraw his candidacy, he was then threatened by the city prosecutor with criminal charges for his allegedly slanderous comments about certain members of the local elite made at a recent party conference in the city. In order to counter these intimidations from above, the labour collective that initially proposed his candidacy met a second and then a third time to reaffirm his nomination. This support from the factory floor, along with the publicity given the case in the national press,[69] resulted in Belous' eventual registration as a candidate. In some other cases of a similar type, the CEC intervened directly to overrule the illegal actions of local elites and ensure that duly nominated and, indeed, immensely popular candidates would appear on the ballot.[70] But examples here were few and far between.

The local apparatus seems to have taken a rather dim view of those who sought to exercise the right of nominating candidates at voters' meetings in places of residence. Officials in Arkhangelsk refused a meeting place to one initiative group bearing a petition with the requisite 30 signatures. The group approached the authorities again, this time with a petition containing 300 signatures, but its request for a venue was again denied.[71] Elsewhere, local authorities resurrected now-defunct laws in order to refuse any place of assembly to initiative groups backing candidates not approved by the apparatus, or concocted *ad hoc* (and quite spurious) rulings that negated the results of certain voters' meetings which they had allowed to occur.[72] In the capital, where one might expect a more assiduous observance of the new procedures due to the proximity of both expert advice and the regulatory mechanism of the CEC, local elites in the Tushinskii district flatly refused 'in direct violation of the laws' to acknowledge the candidacies of a number of individuals nominated at residential meetings,[73] while in other quarters of the city they permitted, if not encouraged, right-wing thugs to break up nomination meetings.[74] In Leningrad, an electoral commission announced that it had unilaterally decided to place on the ballot one candidate from among the four nominees who had been put forward.[75]

Although the CEC overruled the actions of the local authorities in a number of instances, the brevity of this phase of the nominations process (in practical terms, about three weeks) resulted in a situation in which the CEC could do little more than shut the proverbial barn door after the horses had bolted.[76] Moreover, the absence of procedures for enforcing the Electoral Law on the very people who were administering it meant that the local apparatus effectively enjoyed the right to violate the law with impunity.[77] This feature of the national elections should be counted among the other concessions offered the apparatus to mollify its resistance to democratization. It amounted to a sort of blanket insurance policy in cases of emergency. If the other concessions, the filters and so forth, proved insufficient in a given instance to control events, this benefaction enabled the apparatus to make up some new rules on the spot in order to do so.

*Pre-electoral District Meetings.* The second battle of the electoral campaign was fought in the trenches of pre-electoral district meetings. Electoral commissions, we recall, possessed the legal right to hold these meetings in those districts in which more than two nominees had been put forward by the voters during the first round of nominations. In some areas, most notably Estonia where the political leadership regarded pre-electoral district meetings as both undemocratic and unnecessary,[78] such meetings were not called. Instead, the names of all those who had been nominated in the first round, regardless of their number, were simply placed on the election ballots. In a few of the districts in which pre-electoral meetings were held, they produced the same result by registering all the nominees, thus leaving the matter of candidate selection solely to the voters.[79] However, in the overwhelming majority of districts in which pre-electoral meetings were conducted, the attrition rate among nominees was high. About two-thirds of the candidates named in the first round failed to survive the second.[80]

In some districts, and these appear to mark the exception rather than the rule, pre-electoral meetings resulted in lively, policy-oriented debates among nominees and delegates alike. Press accounts describe them as veritable models of democracy wherein the delegates were able to transcend their initial personal or organizational attachments and reach decisions on whom to register primarily, if not exclusively, on the grounds of a shared sense of the common good and the arguments put forth by the candidates.[81] Indeed, in at least three instances, it appeared that attempts by the local apparatus to derail the democratic process with intimidation and slander only succeeded in offending the delegates and redoubling their resolve to resist these pressures and make their choices according to the relative merits of the nominees before them.[82]

But, to repeat, cases such as these were the exceptions. The overall pattern would suggest that pre-electoral district meetings provided ample opportunity for local political elites to employ a variety of tactics aimed at eliminating those candidates of whom they disapproved, thereby retaining control over the electoral process or, at least, this phase of it. We might mention, first, in this respect the question of the pre-electoral meetings themselves. The press reported one instance in which such a meeting was not required, inasmuch as only two candidates had been nominated during the initial round. However, since the favourite of the local establishment was not one of them, the apparatus through the electoral commission approached other labour collectives in the district at the eleventh hour with a request that they nominate candidates too. These collectives complied, thereby 'forcing' this same electoral commission to hold a meeting in order to reduce the number of candidates.[83]

Second, the apparatus was usually able to control delegate selection to the pre-electoral meetings. The CEC ruling that at least half of the delegates must be chosen by organizations that had not nominated candidates was especially helpful in this respect. Working through the electoral commissions, local officials could extend invitations to enterprises and institutions whose administrators could be counted on to deliver delegates that would back the candidates of the apparatus, and simply pass over those that might be considered less dependable in this regard. Such tactics enabled electoral commissions to pack these meetings with members and supporters of the local apparatus. The ubiquity of this practice was evinced by the fact that the CEC received over 1,000 complaints on this matter alone.[84] One delegate to a pre-electoral meeting remarked that the affair was not so much a voters' meeting as a gathering of the party-state apparatus and its activists.[85] Sociological research has subsequently shown that the most active group in the population at these meetings was composed of local administrators.[86]

Third, via its control of delegate selection, the apparatus was usually able to dictate the procedures that pre-electoral meetings would follow. This represented an enormous advantage for local elites. A preferred tactic was to dispense with the secret ballot. According to a member of the CEC:

> It happens this way. The prezidium [of the electoral commission] proposes to conduct open voting. And from the audience they shout: 'Let's! Let's!' Well, then, we will have open voting.[87]

As a consequence, individuals would be required in the presence of the local power structure, including their workplace superiors, to register their choices openly.[88] In a number of districts, the adoption of open voting was itself sufficient to secure substantial majorities for the candidates of the apparatus.[89] In places where it was not, the local elite frequently rendered other arbitrary procedural rulings in order to shape outcomes to their benefit. A few shouts of 'enough' from the audience were often sufficient to close debate.[90] Procedural motions from the floor would sometimes be rejected by the authorities without consulting the delegates.[91] In one district in Kiev where a pre-electoral meeting had voted to register three candidates, the presiding officials disappeared for a few minutes to confer on this outcome, then returned with the announcement that only one of the three would have his name entered on the ballot.[92]

Finally, the participants' relative access to the resources required to wage a successful fight to obtain registration as a candidate gave a decisive advantage to the apparatus. Local elites could simply tap the institutions that they managed for personnel, equipment and supplies, and utilize these to generate favourable publicity about their preferred candidates.[93] Equally, as one nominee in Ust'-Kamenogorsk reported, they were not above waging negative campaigns against opponents by circulating rumours and using local newspapers to publish 'insulting' commentary on candidates not to their liking.[94] Access to resources, of course, was an advantage that the apparatus enjoyed on an even broader scale during the electoral campaign.

## THE ELECTION CAMPAIGN

Of the 7,558 candidates initially put forward during the first phase of nominations, 2,895 managed to have their names entered on the ballot by the close of the second. Almost identical numbers of candidates were registered in territorial (1,449) and national-territorial (1,446) districts. The figures presented in Table 1 indicate that two-candidate races were the norm. They also show, however, that the idea of electoral competition had not yet caught on in a considerable number (384) of constituencies, especially those located in Central Asia and the Caucasus.[95]

The period of electoral campaigning that stretched from 23 February until 25 March, the day prior to the national elections, represented a critical phase in the transformation of the Soviet political system. What had been discussed in the press and in journals, what had been resolved at the Nineteenth Party Conference, what had been debated in the autumn and initiated in winter would now be acted out on a mass scale

**Table 1**
*Distribution of Candidates Across Electoral Districts*

| Number of Candidates Registered | Number of Districts |
|---|---|
| 1 | 384 |
| 2 | 953 |
| 3 | 109 |
| 4 | 27 |
| 5 | 12 |
| 6 | 7 |
| 7 | 4 |
| 8, 9, 11, or 12 | 1 in each case |

*Source:* I. Karpenko, 'Nachalis' vybory narodnykh deputatov SSSR', *Izvestiya* (11 Mar. 1989).

by the entire Soviet population. Real elections. Democracy. And more: an open struggle between the old guard and an emergent popular leadership that steadily grew accustomed to speaking in the name of the people and against the ruling apparatus, its unconscionable privileges, its incompetence and its abuse of power.

The contest for office unfolded, of course, differently in different places. In less politically developed areas, the new elections very much resembled the old ones. In Kazakhstan, all 17 obkom first secretaries stood for office unopposed and all were elected.[96] In the more advanced regions such as the Baltic, however, intense competition broke out between the apparatus and the (by now) well-organized popular movements.[97] Indeed, the electoral campaign provided an unprecedented opportunity for opposition groups to focus their organizing efforts, concentrate their energies on a clear and specific goal and bring their ideas to the larger public. In Leningrad, for instance, dozens of small groups concerned mainly with problems of ecology and the preservation of historic places had long been targets of heavy repression by the local authorities.[98] The elections gave them the chance to strike back by joining forces behind sympathetic candidates and working against those representing the local power structure.[99] They did so on a broad scale and with devastating results for the local elite.

Sociological research has demonstrated that in the more developed areas of the USSR, independent political groups such as those in Leningrad played an important, even decisive, role in the election campaigns. About one-half of those elected in the more advanced regions claimed that victory was achieved in the face of opposition from the local apparatus, and most voters identified informal political groups as the ones who conducted 'energetic, intelligent and honourable' campaigns.[100] The intensity of the electoral contest, a head-to-head struggle for power between the apparatus and the emergent democratic forces, was epitomized by events in Minsk where the police administered beatings to peacefully assembled pickets, gaoled scores of them, and carried out numerous illegal raids on the offices of independent political groups, confiscating their materials and destroying their property.[101] But it was in Moscow that the grand drama of the elections unfolded.

*Moskovskaya tribuna*, which had come into existence in October, surfaced early in the electoral process as the leading voice among democratically-oriented intellectuals in the Soviet capital. Many of its more prominent members were invited by the weekly, *Moscow News*, to take part in the 'social council' that the newspaper was organizing to work out an election platform that reflected the views of its readership.[102] Subsequently, the 'radical-democratic' programme adopted by the social council was promulgated by the newspaper as a common platform for a number of Moskovskaya tribuna members who were campaigning for office.[103] By early February when it was officially chartered, Moskovskaya tribuna was assuming the character of an opposition party in embryo, complete with an illustrious leadership, a distinct political programme,[104] its own press outlet, and organizational links to opposition movements in the Baltic and Armenia.[105] A new and decisive stage in the development of an opposition was reached when this group unofficially joined forces with a political leader capable of igniting the larger public, Boris El'tsin.

As a public figure, El'tsin's stature had been enhanced by the very apparatus that had sought to undo him. His demotion from the post of First Secretary of the Moscow City Committee of the Communist Party to that of First Deputy President of the State Committee on Construction, concomitant with the loss of his seat on the Politburo, was widely interpreted as the consequences of a political struggle over the pace and fate of *perestroika* in which conservative forces had momentarily, at least, consolidated their position by expelling their most prominent opponent from the inner circle of power.

The elections afforded El'tsin a new forum in which to continue his assault on the conservatives entrenched in the apparatus. After having been excluded from the list of candidates selected by the Communist Party to fill its 100 seats on the Congress of People's Deputies, El'tsin was reportedly advised by senior party officials to stay out of the elections altogether.[106] He chose, however, to stand for election in the country's most prominent district, Moscow's national-territorial district No. 1, which encompasses the entire capital and includes nearly six million voters. During the campaign, El'tsin's opponents in the apparatus seemed to spare no effort to make life difficult for him. They disrupted the production of his campaign literature,[107] distributed anonymous pamphlets that viciously attacked his character,[108] placed threatening phone calls to his home and damaged his property,[109] and organized an inquisition in the form of a special subcommission of the party's Central Committee charged with determining whether El'stin should be expelled from the party because of the views that he was expressing.[110] All of this backfired splendidly. The more the conservatives attacked El'tsin, the larger and more enthusiastic became the crowds he drew as he stumped around Moscow.[111]

The ineptitude of the conservatives reached its apogee on 19 March when some 5,000 El'tsin supporters gathered in Gorky Park to stage a campaign rally that had received official sanction from the city authorities.[112] No sooner had a crowd assembled when a sizable cohort of police appeared on the scene to inform them that the Moscow City Soviet had changed its mind about the rally, that their demonstration was now illegal and that they must disperse at once. Brilliantly, the rally's organizers turned this apparent setback to their own advantage. They led the crowd on foot to the offices of the Moscow City Soviet in order to demand an explanation from the authorities for the rally's cancellation. As the crowd, waving placards and chanting slogans, marched the two miles through the capital's central districts to the City Soviet, thousands of Muscovites came off the pavements to join them in the street. Their numbers thus swelled to some 10,000 by the time they reached their destination. Emboldened by this spontaneous display of public support and, perhaps equally, by the timidity of the authorities (none of whom would leave the fortress-like confines of the City Soviet to meet with the demonstrators) the crowd decided to continue its rally there on Gorky Street. For El'tsin's supporters, the symbolism of the ensuing event could scarcely have been more poignant. Traffic was stopped on Gorky Street for the remainder of the day. In front of their City Soviet, through whose windows some of El'tsin's most bitter foes helplessly looked on in dismay, the people of Moscow staged a celebration of democracy.

The El'tsin campaign underscored the only aspect of the nationwide elections that appeared to be clear and unmistakable, namely, the breadth and depth of public opposition to the ruling apparatus. In the context of the political reawakening under way in Soviet society, El'tsin tapped an enormous reservoir of popular discontent simply by repeatedly reminding the voters of one incontrovertible fact: those who are ruling badly are living well. The success that he and other left-democratic candidates enjoyed seemed primarily attributable to a mood among the voters of unqualified opposition to the apparatus and all that it symbolized. These feelings surfaced clearly in a nationwide survey conducted during the election campaign in which respondents, when asked to identify the negative traits of candidates, most frequently named those with wealth and those in the apparatus.[113]

As we have seen, the apparatus enjoyed tremendous advantages in registering their preferred candidates and in keeping opponents off the ballot. During the campaign, these advantages continued. In consonance with their longstanding proclivity to treat state property as their private preserve, the apparatus was able to throw considerable resources—personnel, printing equipment and supplies, transportation and so forth—behind their own candidates[114] and to toss spanners into the campaign machinery of those competing against them.[115] Yet the simple message of 'social justice' voiced by El'tsin and others on the democratic left proved sufficient on election day to overcome these advantages and to hand the apparatus a string of humiliating defeats.[116]

Other aspects of the campaign, however, are difficult, if not impossible, to discern. Take, for instance, the question of campaign programmes, their relative appeal to the electorate and the resulting mandate to govern with which democratic elections (at least in principle) are associated. Was the Soviet electorate concerned with specific political issues? Did voters prefer candidate $X$ to candidate $Y$ because of his programme? Did the election campaign register a set of priority issues among the public that victorious candidates could then carry as a popular mandate into the legislature and enact as public policy? The nature of these elections prevents us from answering any of these questions in the affirmative. This is not to say that the voters were unconcerned with issues, that candidates did not put forward platforms, or that those who were ultimately elected did not represent the wishes of their constituents in the legislature. Rather, the interpretation here is that the national elections occurred within a context similar to that of the nationwide assessment of the Constitutional amendments, and that this context tended to blur and confuse the matter of issues, programmes and mandates.

In fact the election campaign generated a surfeit of ostensible programmes. During the initial stage of candidate nominations, the Central Committee of the Communist Party issued a platform intended to serve as a basis for the campaigns of all party members seeking election.[117] In its vagueness, it more resembled a litany of good works, either currently under way or in the process of formulation, than a party programme *per se*. It contained no reference to policy choices, except in the trivial sense of endorsing the 'good' over the 'bad'. It included no mention of how its splendid and often mutually exclusive goals (more production plus a cleaner environment, more economic efficiency plus more funding for pensions and public health and so forth) were to be realized. Consequently, it would be difficult, and probably mistaken, to regard this document as an election platform in the proper sense of the term.

During the nominations period and the electoral campaign, all candidates put forward their own, individual platforms. While these were often quite specific on the issues[118] and widely promulgated through the mass media[119] and at voters' meetings, they too cannot be regarded as relevant to the question of voter choice among competing electoral programmes. On the one hand, the absence of opposing parties rendered moot the question of programmatic competition. Since each of these platforms represented the proposals of a single candidate, rather than a programme that a party has collectively pledged to work for in the legislature, the question of the responsibility of candidates as would-be legislators simply did not apply. Whereas political parties might be held accountable to the voters for delivering on the promises contained in their platforms (a responsibility that would affect the content of the platforms themselves) such cannot be the case for candidates running individually, for the obvious reason that no individual candidate, if elected, could enact his programme himself. During the campaign, then, no candidate was required to defend the platform of his group or attack that of his opponents. Consequently, such novelties as candidates' debates at voters' meetings or on television almost invariably witnessed the contenders talking past one another, except to exchange compliments and engage in mutual flattery.[120] And this aspect of the campaign, the absence of genuine programmatic competition, was not lost on the electorate themselves. A mass survey conducted by the Scientific Research Institute of the Academy of Social Sciences disclosed that 60 per cent of the voters regarded the platforms of the candidates as collections of unrealistic promises that would not be fulfilled were these candidates elected.[121]

Finally, we have the voters themselves, 34 per cent of whom were reported during the campaign to be prepared to vote for whomever the authorities instructed them to support. Among two-thirds of the electorate not voting blindly, the most important criterion relied upon was the personal qualities of the candidates. As far as issues were concerned, local problems, rather than questions of national policy, headed the list.[122] Indeed, faced with the Communist Party's unified but vacuous platform at one end, and the thousands of isolated programmes offered by individual candidates at the other, it is difficult to imagine the electorate behaving in any other way. Hence, the message sent by the voters on election day on the matter of issues and policy represented the complement to the Communist Party's campaign platform. The former was as fractured as the latter was abstruse.

These shortcomings in the electoral campaign would seem to be wholly traceable to the Communist Party's monopoly on political power. In fact, the campaign itself tended to subvert that monopoly and, in the process, reveal something of import with respect to the nature of the Communist Party itself; namely, that it is not at all a political party in any meaningful sense of the term. The campaign platform that it issued was for all intents and purposes simply irrelevant to the actual competition among candidates; in the overwhelming majority of instances, members of same 'party' stood in opposition to one another for seats in the legislature; nearly half (44 per cent) of the members of the Communist Party negatively evaluated the activities of their own party committees in the elections.[123] The exception that would show this rule was provided by the Baltic republics where popular fronts had organized themselves in opposition to the entrenched apparatus. Consequently, the election campaigns in these republics were distinguished from all others in the country. They involved the relatively clear issues of national identity, self-rule and economic autonomy. They yielded electoral mandates that were carried into the legislature by organized contingents of deputies and, as we see below, produced new legislation in these areas for the republics concerned. Elsewhere, however, due to the lack of such political organization, the Communist Party continued to function as it had for some 70 years as a form of un-party or even anti-party, i.e., that which prevents the political organization of society, that which disorganizes the electorate.

Prior to the political transformation launched at the Nineteenth Party Conference, this anti-party character of the Communist Party was in some respects obscured by its method of rule. The Communist Party simply dictated to society a political agenda and suppressed any and all alternatives. Unfortunately, a number of Western analysts took quite seriously Lenin's statement that this was a 'party of a new type', and, accordingly, provided it with labels such as 'totalitarian party', 'party of mass mobilization' and so forth. Perhaps the closest any came to discovering the truth about it occurred in those instances in which analysts chose to call it by a new name (e.g., 'mafia'). With a change in context from single-candidate elections to competitive ones, however, we notice a concomitant change in its method of rule. This has highlighted what had previously been the underside of its positive posture of activity, viz., the primary political function of this organization is a negative one. It prevents the formation of political parties. In the past, simple repression was sufficient to accomplish this purpose. In the period of *perestroika*, however, its method has changed to allow a pluralism of opinion to express itself beneath the expansive umbrella of permitted speech that it has provided. But this change of method is not without consequences. Indeed, the question arises as to how long the Communist Party might retain its monopoly of political power when some of its own members stand for public office and are elected on programmes that advocate the creation of a multi-party system.[124] It is perhaps in the nature of transition periods such as the one under consideration here that that which is in the process of becoming remains unclear and difficult to apprehend, while that which is passing shows itself full-face for the first time.

# ELECTION RESULTS

High voter turnout was the first significant result of the national elections. In the past, the authorities had relied upon a combination of persuasion, coercion, illegal practices and outright fraud to post incredibly high rates of participation in excess of the 99 per cent mark. These methods were effectively abandoned in the elections of 26 March,[125] and citizens were at liberty to refrain from voting if they so chose. Yet 89.8 per cent of the electorate turned out to cast their ballots.[126] The highest levels of voter turnout (in the upper 90 per cent range) were recorded in Central Asia and the Caucasus (although an organized electoral boycott in Armenia restricted participation there to 71.9 per cent) where single-candidate races were still the norm. But the figures from other parts of the country where multi-candidate races were most commonly held were more than respectable, ranging from 82.5 per cent in Lithuania to 93.4 per cent in the Ukraine.[127]

In view of our discussion of the confusion that surrounded the matter of candidates' platforms and the inability of the electorate to signify clearly its preferences on the issues, we pass over the question of what the vote may have meant from the perspective of the policy orientations of the electorate. Suffice it to say that this aspect of the elections resembled the nationwide assessment and public debate on the Constitutional amendments of the preceding autumn. Individuals in either case may have been free to speak their minds, but neither they nor we have any way of knowing whether someone in authority was listening and, moreover, whether that someone could and would act on the advice of the speakers. With the exception of the Baltic republics where popular fronts were able to organize the electorate around the issue of regional autonomy, the only consensus produced by the elections was an endorsement of all good things—more production, more social benefits, more environmental protection and so forth.

But unlike the Constitutional assessment, the elections gave the public a direct voice. They could vote. Even in those constituencies in which only one candidate had been nominated, voters were required by law to mark their ballots in secret and, protected by the privacy of the voting booth, they could strike off that one name with impunity if they so desired. Particularly in those areas where a more developed political culture prevailed, the voters used their new electoral rights to deliver a series of surprising[128] and often crushing defeats to the apparatus and

their preferred candidates. In addition to the 76 run-off elections occasioned by the absence of a clear majority for any candidate in fields
of three or more, new elections were forced in 199 districts in which a
majority of the voters had crossed off either the name of the single
candidate standing for the seat or the names of both of the candidates
competing in that district.[129]

The most spectacular of the electoral outcomes was Boris El'tsin's
victory over Evgenii Brakov, director of Moscow's ZIL Automotive
Plant. El'tsin, the premier anti-apparatus candidate, captured an as-
tounding 89 per cent of the 5.7 million votes cast in this contest, while
his well-financed opponent failed to reach the seven per cent mark.[130]
The El'tsin phenomenon surely contributed to the success of a number
of other left-democratic candidates in the capital who spared no effort
to associate their candidacies with his,[131] and to the defeat of Moscow's
Mayor, Valerii Saikin, who was running in one of the territorial districts.[132] It also became a *cause celebre* in the run-off and repeat
elections that ensued, with voters regularly quizzing the candidates
about their relation to Boris El'tsin.[133]

In Leningrad, the apparatus was decimated at the polls. Yu. F.
Solov'ev, First Secretary of the Leningrad Obkom, ran unopposed and
was favoured by some voting booth irregularities that compromised the
secrecy of the ballot.[134] Over 60 per cent of the voters, however, struck
off his name.[135] A. N. Gerasimov, First Secretary of the Leningrad
Gorkom, managed to capture only 15 per cent of the vote, losing to Yurii
Boldyrev, a shipbuilding engineer and member of the political group,
Leningrad Perestroika.[136] The remaining four top officials in the
region—the Mayor and Deputy Mayor of Leningrad, the President of
the Regional Soviet and the Second Secretary of the Leningrad
Obkom—were also all defeated at the polls. The voters in Leningrad
seem to have responded readily to the city wide leafleting campaign,
conducted by a number of political groups who had joined forces under
the name, 'Elections '89', that had urged them to strike from their
ballots the names of all those in the local elite.[137]

Elsewhere around the country, a number of prominent members of
the apparatus also experienced humiliating defeats. All of the party's
166 regional first secretaries stood for election, usually unopposed, and
33 of them were rejected by the voters.[138] Portentously, this latter
group included all of the party leaders in the mining regions of the Urals
and Western Siberia that would be rocked by a wave of strikes within

a few months.[139] In Kiev, both the Mayor and the First Secretary of the Gorkom ran in uncontested races and lost.[140] The same was true of the First Secretary in the city of Lvov.[141] In Zhitomir, Alla Yaroshyns'ka, whose candidacy was only made possible by CEC intervention that over-ruled the massive illegalities in the nominations process perpetrated there by the local apparatus, captured 90.4 per cent of the vote.[142] In Belorussia, two regional party first secretaries, the First Secretary of the Minsk Gorkom, the President of the Mogilev Regional Soviet and the First Deputy Chairperson of the Belorussian Council of Ministers all suffered defeats. Two of the Republic's leading industrial directors, M. Lavrinovich of the Belorussian Automotive Works and A. Zinkevich of the Minsk Ballbearing Plant, faced off in a two-man race and were both rejected by the voters.[143]

In the Baltic republics, the popular fronts followed a strategy of running their own candidates in all but a few districts in which officials of the party or state sympathetically disposed toward the fronts were standing for election. The returns in each republic witnessed landslides for the popular front candidates or those whom they had endorsed. With the exception of First Secretary of the Latvian Communist Party, Janis Vargis, who managed by a slender margin (51.3 per cent) to secure victory, the elections resulted in a string of defeats for candidates from the apparatus; these included the Chairperson of the Latvian Council of Ministers, the First Secretary of the Riga Gorkom, the Second Secretary of the Estonian Communist Party, the President of the Lithuanian Supreme Soviet and the Chairperson of the Lithuanian Council of Ministers.[144]

Elections continued until the very eve of the Congress of People's Deputies, its opening postponed by a month in order to allow the electoral process to run its course. Some 150 candidates competed for 76 seats in the run-off elections held in early April, which involved the top two vote-getters in each district in which no candidate (in a field of three or more) had received a majority in the balloting of 26 March. Due to an anomaly in the Electoral Law, it was possible for candidates in this round to win a seat without getting a majority of the vote, and in a few districts in which a majority struck the names of both candidates from the ballot, this actually occurred.[145] Voter participation in this round was somewhat lighter (74.5 per cent) than in the first one, but some of the contests were no less interesting. The popular fronts in the Baltic continued to score victories. In Moscow, the election of such candidates as Roy Medvedev, the outspoken Marxist historian who was the subject of repression in the pre-Gorbachev period, and Sergei Stankevich of Moscow's Popular Front, added to the new legislature's left-democratic column.

The repeated elections, required in those 198 districts in which one- or two-candidate races on 26 March had produced no winners, got under way with a new round of nominations during the first half of April. In proportion to the number of seats under contention, the number of candidates eventually registered (1,216) for the new balloting of 14 May was about twice as many as previously. In 15 of the districts only one candidate appeared on the May ballot, but, in 127 districts, four or more were included, with numbers at the upper end of the scale (25 for one seat in Kishinev, 33 in Kiev, 34 in Leningrad) reaching unwieldy dimensions.[146] Consequently, run-off elections were subsequently required in 125 of these districts.[147] Voter turnout in this round, perhaps hampered by unseasonably warm weather and the lure of a weekend at the dacha, only reached the 78.4 per cent mark.[148]

Since the May elections were the direct result of the voters' rejection of all the candidates placed before them in March, it appeared that many in the apparatus, having been caught off guard by the previous outcome, now redoubled their efforts to ensure the desired results this time around. Local press campaigns were mounted in a number of districts to libel anti-apparatus candidates,[149] while in others the authorities engaged in some rather coarse violations of the electoral procedures in order to prevent the nomination of opponents.[150] In one such instance in Ryazan, local officials denied the petition of a group of 'greens' who had requested the use of a hall in which to hold a voters' meeting to nominate their candidate. On the following day, the greens and their supporters staged a peaceful demonstration outside the city soviet as their leaders negotiated with the authorities inside the building. Suddenly, the police attacked the crowd with truncheons, injuring many and arresting some 30 of the demonstrators. Medical attention was withheld from those detainees who had been injured in the beatings, and a number of the demonstrators were handed short jail-terms and fines for allegedly inciting others to violence.[151]

In the Irkutsk Region, an open struggle broke out within the apparatus itself. There, a candidate was subjected to threats and intimidation by the First Secretary of the Raikom, along with others from the apparatus of the Obkom who were acting unofficially as campaign staff for another candidate. Malicious rumours were circulated about his character and exceptionally unflattering articles about him began to appear in the local press. However, other party and soviet officials in the locale came to his aid and succeded in calling a meeting of the district committee at which the tactics of the First Secretary were condemned. A letter to this effect, signed by 20 members of the Raikom, was subsequently endorsed by the Irkutsk Obkom and published in the regional press.[152]

Such instances of police violence and open struggle within the apparatus indicated how much was at stake in these elections. Not only did high-ranking officials face and, often enough, experience the humiliation of rejection at the hands of the voters, but their positions in the apparatus and, by implication, those of their clients were also at risk. In his address to representatives of the mass media delivered shortly after the balloting in March, Gorbachev spoke of the defeats suffered by party officials as the outcome of 'a normal process, a democratic one, that we must not regard as some kind of tragedy'. He went on to note that these defeats were 'signals to the Central Committee and to [the respective] party committees concerning cadres policy'.[153] In short, failure to win a public election might suffice to remove one's name from the *nomenklatura*.

When the Central Committee of the Communist Party convened in plenary session on 25 April, this daunting prospect provoked a sharp reaction from a number of conservatives who spoke of the democratization under way in Soviet society as the root cause of all the difficulties, real or imagined, that currently beset the country. V. I. Mel'nikov, First Secretary of the Komi Obkom and himself a successful candidates in the March elections, warned of an impending boycott by the apparatus of the republic and local elections scheduled for the autumn. 'Today', he said, 'secretaries of city and district party committees are announcing that they are not going to take part in these elections because there is a 100 per cent guarantee that they will not be elected.'[154]

Despite the cascade of protest issuing from Central Committee conservatives, the Plenum represented a moment of triumph for the reform leadership. Against the backdrop of the election debacles experienced by many leading figures in the apparatus, 74 members and 36 candidate-members of the Central Committee who had retired from their full-time posts over the past three years tendered their resignations from that body, thus radically shifting the balance of power in the

Central Committee in favour of the progressives.[155] In his concluding remarks, Gorbachev repeatedly referred to the election results as a mandate for *perestroika* and, by implication, as something of a vote of 'no confidence' in the ruling apparatus whose conservative elements he likened to military commanders who have remained behind sitting in their bunkers, while the troops whom they are supposed to lead are conducting the offensive on their own. With the elections, he argued, *perestroika*, begun on initiative 'from above', has reached 'a decisive stage characterized by a powerful movement from below—a movement of the broadest mass of working people'.[156]

In retrospect, it would appear that the architects of democratization in the USSR had been wagering on the emergence of this movement all along. Although the compromises that they had struck with conservatives had equipped the apparatus with a formidable protective armour to deflect the challenges of the democratic forces (the 'filters' contained in the Constitutional amendments and Law on Elections, the relative absence of safeguards against manipulation of the nominations process and electoral campaigns by the local apparatus), a weapon of even greater consequence had been placed in the hands of the people—the opportunity to vote by secret ballot. In using this weapon, the citizenry for the first time entered the arena in which the struggle for democratization was being fought out. Never mind that their numbers were not proportionately reflected in the composition of the new legislature. The weight of their numbers stood behind those entering the Congress with the avowed aim of extending the process of democratization, in part by removing the anti-democratic features of the initial compromise.

## NOTES

1. V. Kadzhaya, 'Takoe nelegkoe vzroslenie', *Sovety narodnykh deputatov*, (April, 1989), p. 33; see also the editoral ' Voskhozhdenie k narodovlastiyu', *Ogonek*, No. 11 (11-18 Mar. 1989), p.1; 'Zayavlenie', Council of Seim, Lithuanian Movement for Perestroika (24 Feb. 1989), *Vozrozhdenie*, No. 9 (3 Mar. 1989), p. 5.
2. The heat generated by this struggle was visible in the rather intemperate remarks made about leaders of the democratic oppostion by Politburo member, V. M. Chebrikov, during his speech in Kishinev. 'Predvybornaya platforma partii—real'nyi put' uglubleniya perestroiki', *Pravda* (11 Feb. 1989).
3. V. Orlov, 'Tsentrizbirkom deistvuet', *Sovety narodnykh deputatov*, (Feb., 1989), p. 29.

4. One member of the CEC mentioned during an interview that his election was secured by Vice-President A. I. Luk'yanov, who telephoned party officials within a trade union instructing them to nominate him.
5. Interview (6 May 1989).
6. Orlov, 'Tsentrizbirkom', p. 31.
7. M. Kushtapin, 'Tsentral'naya izbiratel'naya komissiya pristupila k rabote', *Izvestiya* (8 Dec. 1988).
8. Orlov, 'Tsentrizbirkom', p. 29.
9. Yu. I. Ryzhov, interviewed by V. Saklakov, 'Deputat dlya perestroiki', *Izvestiya* (29 Dec. 1988).
10. See the interview with V. P. Orlov, *Izvestiya* (11 Dec. 1988).
11. One member of the CEC stated during a subsequent interview that the selection of the electoral commissions provided the apparatus with the opportunity to steal a march on everyone else by ensconcing their people in these crucial postions before the public was aware of what was going on. For a published account of this phenomenon, see Arno Al'mann, 'Aktual'nye politicheskie voprosy', *Kommunist Estonii*, No. 2 (1989), pp. 97-102.
12. I. Fonyakov, 'Ravnodushnykh net', *Literaturnaya gazeta*, No. 2 (11 Jan. 1989), p.10.
13. For example, see the letter from G. Obrezkov, 'Izbrany dlya podpisi?', *Izvestiya* (16 Jan. 1989).
14. Quoted in V. Tolstenko, 'Kollektiv otstoyal svoego pretendenta', *Izvestiya* (13 Feb. 1989).
15. M. Kushtapin, 'Mandaty dostalis' ne vsem', *Izvestiya* (22 Dec. 1988).
16. Interview with G. V. Barabashev (7 May 1989).
17. See, for example, the account in *Argumenty i fakty*, No. 5 (4-10 Feb. 1989), p. 2; Orlov, 'Tsentrizbirkom', pp. 31-32.
18. I. Karpenko, 'Vremya predvybornykh vstrech', *Izvestiya* (1 Mar. 1989).
19. 'Agitatsiya bez agitpunktov', *Izvestiya* (4 Feb. 1989).
20. I. Karpenko, 'V Tsentral'noi izbiratel'noi komissii', *Izvestiya* (15 Feb. 1989).
21. Interview with G. V. Barabashev (8 May 1989).
22. I. Karpenko, 'V Tsentral'noi izbiratel'noi komissii', *Izvestiya* (1 Feb. 1989).
23. V. Dolganov, 'Vremya vybora', *Izvestiya* (13 Mar. 1989).
24. See the communique published in *Pravda* and *Izvestiya* (10 Dec. 1988).
25. Gorbachev provided these data in his report to a Plenum of the Central Committee on 10 January 1989.
26. Boris Nikol'skii, 'Smotret' pravde v glaza', *Vechernii Leningrad* (6 Apr. 1989).
27. 'Deputatskie mandaty partii', *Izvestiya* (6 Mar. 1989).
28. *Izvestiya* (19 Mar. 1989).
29. Orlov, 'Tsentrizbirkom', p. 33.
30. Stephen White, 'Soviet Elections: From Acclamation to Limited Choice' (mimeo; Glasgow: University of Glasgow, 1989), pp. 7-8.
31. Nikolai Pal'tsev, interviewed by Yuliya Khaitina, 'Tri dnya do finisha', *Moskovskii komsomolets* (14 Mar. 1989).
32. Quoted in Kadzhaya, 'Takoe nelegkoe vzroslenie', p. 31.
33. A. Stepovoi, 'Komitet sovetskikh zhenshchin', *Izvestiya* (22 Mar. 1989).
34. See the results published in *Izvestiya* (25 Mar. 1989).
35. White, 'Soviet Elections ...', p. 6.
36. V. Dolganov, 'Izbrany pervye narodnye deputaty SSSR', *Izvestiya* (12 Mar. 1989).
37. M. Kushtapin, 'Pyat' mandatov—pyat' pretendentov', *Izvestiya* (12 Jan. 1989).
38. M. Kirsanov, 'Soyuz sovetskikh obshchestv druzhby', *Izvestiya* (22 Mar. 1989).
39. G. Ivanov, 'Kto otstalsya za chertoi,' *Literaturnaya gazeta*, No. 4 (25 Jan. 1989).

40.  Letter to the Editor from R. Sagdeev *et al.*, *Moskovskie novosti*, No. 15 (9 Apr. 1989).
41.  M. Murzina, 'Ne po stsenariyu bylykh vremen', *Izvestiya* (21 Jan. 1989); interview with Anatoli Ilyashov (13 Feb. 1989).
42.  V. Malukhin, 'Debaty pisatelei', *Izvestiya* (20 Jan. 1989).
43.  V. Loganov, 'Po raznym spiskam', *Izvestiya* (12 Jan. 1989).
44.  A Stepovoi, 'Uchimsya vybirat'', *Izvestiya* (27 Dec. 1988).
45.  A. Davydov *et al.*, 'Kandidaty nazvany - bor'ba vpered', *Izvestiya* (25 Jan. 1989).
46.  Andrei Borodenkov, 'Nashim mneniem prenebregli', *Moskovskie novosti*, No. 7 (12 Feb. 1989); A. Davydov, 'Mandatov bol'she chem pretendentov', *Izvestiya* (20 Jan. 1989).
47.  Borodenkov, 'Nashim mneniem ...'.
48.  V. Dolganov, 'Bez ogladki na prezidium', *Izvestiya* (21 Jan. 1989).
49.  For example, see those from S. I. Mileiko and R. A. Kazantseva, and V. Kunitskii that were published in *Izvestiya* (27 Jan. 1989).
50.  The CEC's official explanation appeared in *Izvestiya* (27 Jan. 1989).
51.  V. Dolganov, 'Miting nauchnoi obshchestvennosti', *Izvestiya* (3 Feb. 1989).
52.  Interview with G. V. Barabashev (6 May 1989); V. Dolganov and M. Kushtapin, 'Akademiya nauk SSSR', *Izvestiya* (22 Mar. 1989).
53.  I. Karpenko, 'Dorogi, kotorymi my vybiraem', *Izvestiya* (21 Mar. 1989).
54.  Dolganov and Kushtapin, 'Akademiya ...'.
55.  V. Dolganov and M. Kushtapin, 'Deputaty ot Akademii nauk SSSR', *Izvestiya* (21 Apr. 1989).
56.  Nominations in military units do not concern us here. The other method of nomination in the districts, namely, by local units of one of the acknowledged public organizations, was only employed in one instance. In that case, the Novosibirsk chapter of the All-Union Volunteer Society for the Struggle for Sobriety sought to place 20 names in nomination for seats in Moscow and Leningrad. Although the Law on Elections does not expressly forbid such practices, the CEC denied the Novosibirsk application on the grounds that it would be impossible to legislate for all eventualities (hence, the Law as written did not cover such a case) and that the spirit of the law suggested that nominations by local organizations should refer to the locality in which they operated (the alternative, by which any local organization could nominate candidates anywhere, was regarded as an invitation to chaos). Of some relevance to this case was the fact that Pamyat', the right-wing extremist organization, was apparently attempting to register its candidates in Moscow and Leningrad through this circuitous route involving its control of the Novosibirsk branch of the Society for the Struggle for Sobriety. Interview with G. V. Barabashev (6 May 1989).
57.  Karpenko, 'Dorogi, kotorymi ...'.
58.  Karpenko, 'V Tsentral'noi ...'. (1 Feb. 1989).
59.  White, 'Soviet Elections ...'.
60.  A. Stepovoi, 'Brateevskii fenomen', *Izvestiya* (26 Jan. 1989). This candidate, however, was subsequently removed from contention at a pre-electoral district meeting. E. Andryushchenko, interviewed by V. Voronetskii, 'Vybory: uroki i tendentsii', *Argumenty i fakty*, No. 19 (13-19 May 1989), pp. 1-2.
61.  For examples of this phenomenon, see V. Nikolaeva, 'Luchshego—iz odnogo', *Izvestiya* (14 Jan. 1989).
62.  E.g., V. Kulagin, 'Po vcherashnim retseptam', *Izvestiya* (24 Jan. 1989); V. Solyanik, 'Vetry peremen i starye prepony', *Sovety narodnykh deputatov*, (Feb., 1989), pp. 36-38; 'V tekh zhe dvukh okrugakh', *ibid.* (Mar., 1989), pp. 27-30.

63. Andrei Nuikin, 'Stat' deputatom', *Moskovskie novosti*, No. 10 (5 Mar. 1989), p. 13.
64. V. Voblikov, 'V zashchitu svoei kandidatury? Net! V zashchitu perestroiki', *Izvestiya* (20 Jan. 1989).
65. Tolstenko, 'Kollektiv otstoyal ...'.
66. V. Istomin, 'Skazka dlya izbiratelei', *Leningradskaya pravda* (17 Jan. 1989); Andrei Romanov, 'Po 132-i stat'e', *Moskovskie novosti*, No. 9 (26 Feb. 1989), p. 13
67. Aleksandr Bolotin and Lev Sherstennikov, 'Raskovanost', *Ogonek*, No. 7 (Feb., 1989), pp. 1-2.
68. L. Annus, 'O glasnosti—glasno ...', *Sovetskaya Estoniya* (23 Feb. 1989).
69. Letter from N. Belous, 'Pochemu ya otkazalsya ot samootvoda', *Izvestiya* (10 Jan. 1989); A. Solov'ev, 'Izbirateli podderzhali', *ibid.* (30 Jan. 1989).
70. CEC member, G. V. Barabashev, recounted in an interview (5 May 1989) two particularly dramatic interventions on the part of the CEC to uphold legal procedures in the face of apparatus attempts to steamroller opponents. One involved miners at the Fifty Years of the October Revolution mining complex near Donetsk who staged a sustained protest when their preferred candidate was arbitrarily de-registered in order to leave the field open to the other nominee, V. A. Masol, Chairperson of the Ukrainian Council of Ministers. The other referred to a popular journalist, Alla Yaroshyns'ka, who faced continual obstruction and harassment from the apparatus in Zhitomir where she worked. In both cases, CEC intervention was sufficient to nullify local machinations and secure candidate status for the nominees. Indeed, for Yaroshyns'ka, the exposure of apparatus wrongdoing during the nominations and election campaign (including the arbitrary arrest of some of her supporters) apparently resulted in a resounding victory for her at the polls on 26 March. On this episode, see Kathleen Mihalisko, 'Alla Yaroshyns'ka: Crusading Journalist from Zhitomir Becomes People's Deputy', *Radio Liberty Report on the USSR*, RL 247/89 (24 May 1989), pp. 17-19.
71. S. Novitskii, 'Zhdut komandy iz tsentra', *Izvestiya* (19 Jan. 1989).
72. See the telegrams published by *Izvestiya* (20 Jan. 1989).
73. A. Davydov *et al.*, 'Kandidaty nazvany—bor'ba vperedi', *Izvestiya* (25 Jan. 1989). I. Korolikov reported on similar mischief made by local district authorities throughout Moscow. In some instances, initiative groups were denied meeting places on the basis of defunct decrees; in others, they were refused the use of them because of the particular candidates they intended to nominate. See his 'My tak schitaem', *ibid.* (17 Jan. 1989).
74. Nuikin, 'Stat' deputatom'; V. Chernov, 'Deti Sharikova', *Ogonek*, No. 3 (Jan., 1989), p. 31.
75. 'Vtoroi etap izbiratel'noi kampanii', *Izvestiya* (28 Jan. 1989).
76. In one case, at least, timely intervention by the CEC did force the local elite to nullify the results of a voters' meeting that they had illegally manipulated and to stage a new meeting at which their own candidate was knocked out of contention. See Renata Verezhanu, 'Nam po silam pobedit byurokratiyu', *Izvestiya* (2 Feb. 1989).
77. Andryushchenko, 'Vybory: uroki i tendentsii', p. 2; Nikol'skii, 'Smotret' pravde v glaza'; Nuikin, 'Stat' deputatom'. For an authoritative statement on this issue, see the interview given by G. V. Barabashev to V. Shchepotkin, 'Volna i krugi', *Izvestiya* (9 Feb. 1989).
78. A.I. Al'mann interviewed by L. Levitskii, 'Bez okruzhnykh sobranii', *Izvestiya* (10 Feb. 1989); Dmitrii Ostal'skii *et al.*, 'Vybor sdelan', *Moskovskie novosti*, No. 14 (2 Apr. 1989).

79. Aivar Baumanis, 'Riga: predvybornye situatsii', *Moskovskie novosti*, No. 9 (26 Feb. 1989).
80. I. Karpenko, 'Nachalis' vybory narodnykh deputatov SSSR', *Izvestiya* (11 Mar. 1989).
81. N. Lisovenko, 'Borolis' na ravnykh', *Izvestiya* (14 Feb. 1989); A. Ershov, 'Kto luchshe zashchit interesy sormovtsev', *ibid.* (17 Feb. 1989); V. Dolganov, 'Spor programm ili konkurs obeshchanii?', *ibid.* (20 Feb. 1989); V. Dolganov, 'Dvoe kandidatov—iz desyati', *ibid.* (23 Feb. 1989); A. Zimova, 'Uroki demokratii', *Mayak* (Moscow Oblast') (18 Feb. 1989); A. Alova, 'S yavnym preimushchestvom', *ibid.* (2 Mar. 1989).
82. S. Kadaurov, 'Kak menya otgovarivali', *Izvestiya* (23 Feb. 1989); A. Karpov, 'Kandidat pred'yavlaet isk', *ibid.*; Nikol'skii, 'Smotret' pravde v glaza'.
83. A. Kleva, 'Vydvizhenets so storony', *Izvestiya* (30 Jan. 1989).
84. Karpenko, 'Dorogi, kotorymi ...'.
85. S. Troyan, 'Nadezhnye lyudi v zale', *Izvestiya* (6 Feb. 1989).
86. V. Levanskii, A. Obolonskii and G. Tokarevskii, 'Chto dumayut lyudi o vyborakh?', *Argumenty i fakty*, No. 10 (11-17 Mar. 1989), p. 2.
87. Barabashev, 'Volna i krugi'.
88. Yu. Perepletkin, 'Pretendentov bylo odinnadtsat'', *Izvestiya* (21 Feb. 1989).
89. Troyan, 'Nadezhnye lyudi v zale'; A. Palat and A. Kleva, 'Kandidaty nachali bor'bu', *Izvestiya* (2 Feb. 1989); A. Krivchenko, 'Edinodushie ravnodushnykh', *ibid.* (14 Feb. 1989); M. Ovcharov and V. Shchepotkin, 'Portret protokola na fone demokratii', *ibid.* (18 Feb. 1989); A. Ivanov, 'Turnir pretendentov: zachem lomalis' kop'ya', *Sovety narodnykh deputatov*, No. 3 (Mar., 1989), pp. 30-32.
90. Barabashev, 'Volna i krugi'.
91. N. Solyanik, 'Porazhenie, ravnoe pobede', *Sovety narodnykh deputatov*, No. 4 (Apr., 1989), pp. 25-27.
92. V. Shchepotkin, 'Vremya gotovit'sya k vyboru', *Izvestiya* (20 Feb. 1989).
93. N. Solyanik, 'Porazhenie, ravnoe pobede'.
94. Letter to the Editor from A. Cherkashina, 'Moi "neugodnyi" kandidat', *Izvestiya* (21 Mar. 1989).
95. Andryushchenko, 'Vybory: uroki i tendentsii', p. 1.
96. *Ibid.*
97. See, for example, the Declaration of the Lithuanian Movement for Perestroika (Sajudis) published in *Vozrozhdenie*, No. 9 (3 Mar. 1989), p. 5.
98. Interview with Elena Zelinskaya, Editor of *Merkurii*, the journal of the cultural-democratic movement known as Epitsentr (17 Nov. 1988). For an account of the police repression visited on activists protesting against the destruction of historic sites in Leningrad during the first days of the nominations stage, see A. Kovalev, 'Arest po ozhegovu', *Stroitel' naya gazeta* (4 Jan. 1989).
99. See the interview given by S. A. Ivanov to A. Manilova, '"Vedu bor'bu chestno"', *Leningradskaya pravda* (7 Apr. 1989).
100. V. Komarovskii and A. Usol'tsev, 'Protivoborstvo? Net, sotrudnichestvo', *Argumenty i fakty*, No. 22 (3-9 June 1989), p. 5.
101. Zenon Poznyak, 'V poslednie predvybornye dni', *Soglasiya*, No. 6 (19 Apr. 1989), p. 8.
102. *Moskovskie novosti*, No. 2 (8 Jan. 1989).
103. 'Predvyborny platformy', *Moskovskie novosti*, No. 4 (22 Jan. 1989), p. 12.
104. Nina Belyaeva, 'Moskovskaya tribuna', *Moskovskie novosti*, No. 7 (12 Feb. 1989).
105. Antaras Burachas, 'Zayavlenie kluba "Moskovskaya tribuna"', *Vozrozhdenie*, No. 10 (10 Mar. 1989), p. 2.
106. White, 'Soviet Elections', p. 11.

107. *Ibid.*
108. Vitalii Tret'yakov, 'Obratnyi effect', *Moskovskie novosti*, No. 12 (19 Mar. 1989).
109. Dawn Mann, 'El'tsin Rides a Political Roller Coaster,' *Radio Liberty Report on the USSR*, RL 253/89 (9 June 1989), p. 13.
110. White, 'Soviet Elections', p. 11.
111. See, for instance, Jonathan Steele, 'Yeltsin wins crowds on the campaign trail', *Manchester Guardian Weekly* (12 Mar. 1989), p. 24.
112. The account of this episode draws on an interview with one of the participants, Vladimir Stratanovich (7 July 1989), and on that of A. Davydov, 'Manifestatsiya i informatsiya', *Izvestiya* (20 Mar. 1989).
113. Levanskii, Obolonskii and Tokarevskii, 'Chto dumayut lyudi o vyborakh?', p. 2.
114. Interview with Barabashev (6 May 1989). See the roundtable discussion, 'Ot real'noi bor'by k real'nym vyboram', *Moskovskie novosti*, No. 11 (12 Mar. 1989).
115. For instance, a journalist reported that a considerable volume of mail had reached his newspaper which complained that, contrary to law, duly registered campaign workers were often denied leave from their jobs in order to carry on campaign activities. See the interview with G. V. Barabashev conducted by V. Shchepotkin, 'Polnomochiya i obyazannosti', *Izvestiya* (14 Mar. 1989).
116. Yurii Orlik reported that 'social justice' and an end to the special privileges of the apparatus were the main issues addressed in letters to his newspaper during the campaign. See his 'O chem pishut rabochie', *Izvestiya* (31 Mar. 1989).
117. 'K partii, sovetskomu narodu', *Sovety narodnykh deputatov*, No. 2 (1989), pp. 3-9.
118. Examples would include S. B. Skvortsov (supported by the Fund for Social Initiative) and S. B. Stankevich (supported by the Moscow Popular Front). The campaign brochures of each are reasonably detailed with respect to the means (taxes, institutional changes, and so forth) for accomplishing certain ends. Stankevich was elected to the Congress of People's Deputies while Skvortsov was not.
119. National, republic and local newspapers throughout the USSR published an enormous amount of material relevant to the candidates and their platforms, usually in the form of interviews in which the candidates would expound on their programmes. The forum of the press was even made available to outright opponents of the Soviet system, such as Einars Repshe of the Movement for the National Independence of Latvia who was interviewed by *Sovetskaya molodezh'* (3 Mar. 1989).
120. On debates at voters' meetings, see Brendan Kiernan, 'Elections to the Congress at People's Deputies: Moscow, 1989' (paper presented at the Social Science Research Council's Summer Workshop, Toronto, Canada, 1989), p. 5. On those broadcast over Soviet television, see V. Dolganov, 'Komplimentarnye pomekhi v debatakh', *Izvestiya* (10 Mar. 1989).
121. V. Komarovskii and E. Dugin, 'Do i posle vyborov', *Izvestiya* (12 May 1989).
122. These data were reported by Levanskii, Obolonskii and Tokarevskii, 'Chto dumayut lyudi o vyborakh?', p. 2. See also N. Popov, 'Obshchestvennoe mnenie i vybory, *Izvestiya* (22 Apr. 1989). Another indication of voter confusion on the question of platforms appeared in the considerable volume of mail subsequently sent to the Mandates Commission of the Congress of People's Deputies that complained not about the procedures under which deputies had been elected—a matter within the purview of that Commission—but about the platform on which they had conducted their campaigns. 'V Mandatnoi komissii S"ezda narodnykh deputatov SSSR', *ibid.* (4 Aug. 1989).
123. Komarovskii and Usol'tsev, 'Protivoborstvo? Net, sotrudnichestvo'.

124. See, for instance, Francis X. Clines, 'Soviet Insurgent Basks in Victory's Glow', *New York Times* (29 Mar. 1989).

125. CEC member G. V. Barabashev reports that fraudulent ballots did turn up in a few places, but their number was insufficient to alter the results of the elections. Interview (6 May 1989).

126. 'Soobshchenie Tsentral'noi izbiratel'noi komissii ob itogakh vyborov narodnykh deputatov SSSR v 1989 godu', *Izvestiya* (5 Apr. 1989).

127. *Ibid.*; Andryushchenko, 'Vybory: uroki i tendentsii', p. 1.

128. One indication of the surprise contained in the election results involves the planned convocation of the Congress of People's Deputies. As late as the first week in March, N. G. Starovoitov, a legal specialist and member of the working group that wrote the Electoral Law, mentioned in an interview that the Congress would meet in April. The large number of run-off elections and repeat elections resulting from the balloting of 26 March, however, caused its postponement until late May. Starovoitov's interview, conducted by Elina Nikolaevna, appeared in *Moskovskii Komsomolets* (5 Mar. 1989).

129. L. Lazerov, interviewed by Dmitrii Ostal'skii, 'Povtornoe golosovanie', *Moskovskie novosti*, No. 15 (9 Apr. 1989).

130. Ester B. Fein, 'Vote Chagrins a Taciturn Soviet Press', *New York Times* (29 Mar. 1989).

131. John Rettle, 'Voters' choice weird but wonderful', *Manchester Guardian Weekly* (9 Apr. 1989); Kiernan, 'Elections to the Congress of People's Deputies', p. 6.

132. Michael Parks, 'Key Soviet Party Officials Defeated', *Los Angeles Times* (28 Mar 1989).

133. V. S. Pasternak, interviewed by V. Vyzhutovich, '"Za i protiv"', *Izvestiya* (6 Apr. 1989).

134. White, 'Soviet Elections', p. 16.

135. Michael Parks, 'Realignment Seen for Soviet Party', *Los Angeles Times* (29 Mar. 1989).

136. *Izvestiya* (27 Mar. 1989).

137. Jonathan Steele, 'Leningrad leads election revolt', *Manchester Guardian Weekly*, (2 Apr. 1989); Bill Keller, 'A Tattered Leningrad Party Wonders What to Do When Voters Say No', *New York Times* (30 March 1989).

138. Interview with Barabashev (6 May 1989). Slightly different figures are mentioned by A. N. Gerasimov in an interview conducted by A. Ezhelev, 'Ponyat', chto proizoshlo', *Izvestiya* (23 Apr. 1989).

139. Jerry F. Hough, 'The Politics of Successful Reform', *Soviet Economy*, Vol. 5, No. 1 (1989), p. 14.

140. 'Utverzhdenie demokratii', *Izvestiya* (28 Mar. 1989).

141. Parks, 'Key Soviet Party Officials Defeated'.

142. Mihalisko, 'Alla Yaroshyns'ka: Crusading Journalist from Zhitomir Becomes People's Deputy', p. 17.

143. 'Utverzhdenie demokratii'.

144. Parks, 'Key Soviet Party Officials Defeated'; Rettle, 'Voters choice weird but wonderful'.

145. 'Itogi povtornogo golosovaniya', *Izvestiya* (15 Apr. 1989).

146. V. Orlov, interviewed by I. Karpenko, 'Pered povtornymi vyborami', *Izvestiya* (5 May 1989).

147. I. Karpenko, 'Nachalos' povtornoe golosovanie', *Izvestiya* (18 May 1989).

148. 'Soobshchenie Tsentral'noi izbiratel'noi komissii ob itogakh povtornykh vyborov narodnykh deputatov SSSR, provedennykh posle 26 marta 1989 goda', *Izvestiya* (20 May 1989).

149. Karpenko, 'Nachalos' povtornoe golosovanie'.
150. V. Dolganov, 'Vybor vo imya peremen', *Izvestiya* (13 May 1989).
151. N. Kiselev, 'U paradnogo pod"ezda', *Komsomolskaya pravda* (26 Apr. 1989).
152. B. Alekseev, 'Kompromat na kandidata', *Izvestiya* (14 Apr. 1989).
153. M. S. Gorbachev, 'Na perelomnom etape perestroiki', *Izvestiya* (29 Mar. 1989).
154. Excerpted in the *New York Times* (28 Apr. 1989).
155. Their collective letter of resignation appeared in *Izvestiya* (26 Apr. 1989).
156. 'Zaklyuchitel'noe slovo M.S. Gorbacheva na Plenume TsK KPSS 25 aprelya 1989 goda', *Izvestiya* (27 Apr. 1989).

# 6. MORE POWER TO THE SOVIETS

This chapter concerns the final phase of the reform project sponsored by the Gorbachev leadership. As such, the events under consideration here represent both an ending and a beginning. The convocation of the Congress of People's Deputies on 25 May 1989 marked the closing stage of democratization from above and, at the same time, opened a new period in Soviet political history. For the debut of the new institutions of government also represented the debut of newly-organized political forces within them who would endeavour to use these institutions to carry forward the process of democratization.

The narrative that follows is intended to straddle this elusive line between past and future. The focus falls on three levels of government and politics in which democratization, initiated from above, has begun to grow over into a process sustained by a movement from below. We take up, firstly, the work of the Congress of People's Deputies and the Supreme Soviet at the national level. Our discussion in this respect is oriented toward the same two basic themes that have guided our investigations of the reform project up to this point, namely, the empowering of legislative institutions and the expansion of their representative (or democratic) content.

Secondly, our attention is directed to developments at the republic level, again with these two themes serving as focal points for the discussion. Inasmuch as political reform at this level has generally lagged behind the changes introduced in the national institutions of government and politics, we survey developments in the Baltic republics where the transition to a democratic political order has advanced furthest. Given the wide range of peoples and cultures that constitute the USSR, it would be foolish to suppose that what is under way in the Baltic today will be repeated elsewhere tomorrow. Yet it would be equally mistaken to believe that the Baltic experience is relevant to that region alone. Rather, the fact that the Baltic republics have taken the lead in asserting their autonomy in political and economic matters represents to others a path already broken, one that they, in their own way of course, might also take.

Finally, we consider what can still be only dimly perceived at this point—the transformation of local soviets into authentic institutions of popular government. More than any other factor, the ultimate success of *perestroika* would seem to hinge on developments at this level. For *perestroika* signifies the replacement of one order, that associated with the 'command-administrative' rule of the party and state apparatuses, by another in which citizens through their own institutions, the soviets, manage their common affairs. If this vision is to be translated into social practice, then no number of decrees from afar, however authoritative, can substitute for the involvement of citizens themselves in institutions of self-government.

## ON THE NATIONAL LEVEL

The data displayed in Table 2 allow us to draw some comparisons between the composition of the Supreme Soviet that was elected in 1984 and that of the newly elected Congress of People's Deputies. Overall, as the sociologists who assembled these data have pointed out,[1] the Congress has a smaller proportion of both top officials and rank-and-file workers than did the old Supreme Soviet, as well as a correspondingly larger percentage of officials working at middle and lower levels in the system (e.g., directors of enterprises and farms). The general categories employed by the Soviet sociologists, however, mask some of these differences. The data set out in Table 3, for instance, show that two categories of top officials, executive officers of the Central Committee and ministers and deputy ministers of the USSR, declined precipitously in the Congress (the latter as a result of the Constitutional provision barring top administrators from serving as deputies in the soviet at the same level), while other groups, such as ministers and deputy ministers in the republics, officials in academic institutions and members of the scientific and creative intelligentsia, increased enormously. Representation of the Communist Party was up from 71.4 per cent in 1984[2] to 87 per cent in 1989[3], while representation of the apparatus of the party was down.[4]

**Table 2**

*Comparative Compositions of the Supreme Soviet Elected in 1984
and the Congress of People's Deputies Elected in 1989\**

|  | Number of Deputies | | In Percentages | |
| --- | --- | --- | --- | --- |
|  | 1984 | 1989 | 1984 | 1989 |
| Top Political Leaders | 23 | 15 | 1.5 | 0.7 |
| Higher and Middle Level Administrators | 599 | 813 | 40.0 | 39.8 |
| Lower Level Administrators | 99 | 504 | 6.6 | 24.7 |
| Workers & Peasants | 688 | 473 | 49.5 | 23.1 |
| Professionals | 90 | 197 | 6.0 | 9.7 |
| Religious Leaders | — | 5 | — | 0.2 |
| Pensioners | — | 37 | — | 1.8 |
| Totals | 1,499 | 2,044 | 100.0 | 100.0 |

*Source:* A. Nazimova and V. Sheinis, 'Vybor sdelan', *Izvestiya* (6 May 1989).

\* These data were compiled before the repeated elections of 1989 had been completed. Consequently, they do not include the final 206 (9.2 per cent) of the deputies elected to the Congress. The results of the repeated elections, however, were generally consistent with the proportions of various categories of members reported here for 1989. The column totals for percentages exceed 100, apparently due to rounding errors.

Owing to the disorganizing effects of the Communist Party's formal monopoly on political power that we discussed in the preceding chapter, the political orientations of the deputies to the Congress are much more difficult to ascertain than are these objectified data concerning their status. Researchers from the Central Committee's Academy of Social Sciences surveyed the opinions of 1,347 deputies on a range of matters pertaining to their work just after the opening days of the Congress. On the basis of their responses, the investigators were able to divide the corpus of legislators into three broad grouping: those with 'radical expectations' for advancing democratic reform, expectations that were little satisfied (25-30 per cent of respondents); a middle group that expected less and was, consequently, more satisfied with the experience of the first days of the Congress's work (40-55 per cent); and those who, out of their own 'more cautious approach', were quite satisfied with the proceedings (15-20 per cent).[5]

The immediate inference suggested by these survey results might be that the Congress was composed of a radical and a conservative wing, with a large group, perhaps a majority, of moderates in the middle. If this indeed represented the subjective orientations of the deputies, then their manifest orientations—that is, what they said and did at the Congress—seemed another matter entirely. The reason for such differences again seems to be the Communist Party and its role in disorganizing political activity. On the one hand, the party did not, and probably could not, unite its members around a common legislative

**Table 3**

*Comparative Compositions of the Supreme Soviet Elected in 1984 and the Congress of People's Deputies Elected in 1989 for Selected Categories*

|  | Number of Debuties | | Overall Percentage of Debuties | |
|---|---|---|---|---|
|  | 1984 | 1989 | 1984 | 1989 |
| Central Committee Executive Officers | 19 | 14 | 1.3 | 0.7 |
| Ministers & Deputy Ministers of the USSR | 90 | 1 | 6.0 | — |
| Leaders of Academies of Science | 18 | 37 | 1.1 | 1.8 |
| Leaders of Scientific Institutes and Higher Schools | — | 83 | — | 4.1 |
| Scientific and Creative Intelligentsia | 27 | 122 | 1.8 | 6.0 |

Source: Nazimova and Sheinis, 'Vybor sdelan'.

programme and enforce voting discipline over them in the legislature.[6] On the other hand, the party continued to prohibit the formation of alternative political parties, thus preventing the self-organization of legislators into clearly-defined political groups. Consequently, what emerged at the Congress was two poles around which the deputies arrayed themselves. One of these was the establishment, so to speak, the political leadership and a large majority of deputies who owed their seats to the anti-democratic mechanics of the electoral system and who had no political programme except to support the Gorbachev leadership against challenges issuing from the second pole, the opposition.

The second pole was itself grounded on two bases of organization that existed before, and were further developed during, the electoral campaigns. One of these bases was regional. It included a majority of the deputies elected in the Baltic who represented the programmes of their respective popular fronts. In the Congress, this group carried out a sustained offensive to enhance and secure the autonomy of their republics. The other organizational nucleus available to those who opposed the establishment on important matters had evolved, firstly, out of Moskovskaya tribuna; thereafter through the organization of left-democratic candidates around the readers' platforms developed by *Moscow News*; and, finally, by means of the alliance worked out between this group and Boris El'tsin during the election campaign. Immediately after the March elections, a number of these left-democratic deputies in Moscow opened an office where they set about the business of drafting a common platform on major issues. Their office was frequented by hundreds of political activists from all quarters of the USSR who offered suggestions and help.[7]

Consigned to minority status by the system under which the deputies were elected, these two opposition groupings tended to make common cause in the Congress against the majority that the Gorbachev leadership was able to muster on every issue. Ironically, the more conservative deputies, owing to their unconcealed distaste for everything that the opposition represented, turned out to be some of Gorbachev's most faithful supporters at the Congress, circling their wagons around the General Secretary, as it were, in order to maintain a large voting majority against any proposal that the opposition put forward. As a consequence of this arrangement, a number of discriminate political orientations present among the deputies, something which under more liberal political circumstances would have led to the formation of a plurality of parliamentary groups (if not separate political parties) remained submerged within the coarser categories of majority and minority.[8]

The legacy of Communist Party rule that had previously functioned on the basis of bogus displays of unanimous public approval for decisions taken behind closed doors by the inscrutable few was particularly evident in the manner in which the Congress conducted its business. Supposedly, the work of the Congress was to be governed by procedures drawn up initially by the Prezidium and then amended at a deputies' conference that was held prior to the opening of the Congress. The procedures distributed to the deputies at the first meeting of the Congress, however, contained none of the amendments adopted at this conference.[9] Indeed, the inattention given by the leadership and the majority to the issue of procedures stalked the entire proceedings like some frightful spectre of political illiteracy giving the lie time and again to winged phrases about constructing a government of laws. The first major order of business at the Congress, for example, was the election of the President of the Supreme Soviet. Although the Constitution specified that the head of the CEC should conduct the meeting of the Congress until the President was elected, Gorbachev simply commandeered this role for himself as soon as the deputies were officially seated. In this capacity, he directed the discussion on the procedures under which the President (namely, himself) would be elected, unilaterally dismissing various proposals from the floor that were not to his liking and inventing a set of election rules apparently on the spot. He was reminded by one deputy, A. V. Levashev, that since his actions in this respect were unconstitutional, his election by the Congress to the post of President would have no legal validity.[10] He facilely waved away this objection too. Indeed, throughout the eleven-day session of the Congress, the absence of clear procedural regulations was evident at every turn. Scores of motions offered from the floor were not put to a vote, while the voting that did occur often resembled what had taken place at the pre-electoral district meetings held during the winter. In either instance, the undifferentiated shouts of approval from the audience in reply to some suggestion put to them by the presiding officer were understood to mean that the rule had been adopted.

In other regards, the proceedings recalled the kitchen-like atmosphere of the public debate that was conducted during the previous autumn. Deputies would rise and speak from their places without the benefit of formal recognition by the presiding officer. The discussion at times seemed especially eclectic, with deputies remarking on whatever happened to be on their minds, regardless of the topic formally under consideration. And in response to statements from the opposition, the more strident members of the majority often attempted to shout down various speakers, openly jeering at them in unsightly displays of ill manners.

During the first few days of the session, most of the Congress's time was spent debating procedural issues. Within the sometimes dry discussions of how voting should be organized, how the schedule of deputies wishing to address the Congress should be composed and so forth, lay the fundamental question of whether the Congress would act as an authentic legislature. Since the deputies could not be organized along party lines, a regional arrangement was adopted whereby the delegations from each of the republics (or, in the case of the large Russian Republic, the delegations from each oblast) composed their own lists of speakers for addressing the Congress and their own slates of nominees for election to the Supreme Soviet.[11] In most cases, members of the apparatus within each of these delegations were able to control the speakers' lists and slates of candidates that the delegations composed.[12] Moreover, since the regional delegations were seated together as groups, and since almost all of the voting at the Congress was accomplished by an open show of hands, members of the apparatus were readily able to observe how their respective delegations voted on the issues.

These arrangements were instrumental in fashioning at the Congress that 'aggressively-obedient majority' about which one member of the democratic opposition openly complained.[13] In order to break the hold that the apparatus held on the great majority of deputies and to enable their own supporters, who comprised minorities in many of the republic and regional delegations, to address the Congress and stand as candidates for election to the Supreme Soviet, members of the opposition introduced a number of procedural proposals. They called, in particular, for roll-call voting on important issues so that constituents would know how their deputies had voted; for adopting the 'competitive principle' in elections to the Supreme Soviet (that is, the idea that each slate of nominees would contain more candidates that there were seats on the Supreme Soviet allotted to the respective delegation) which might enable more of their supporters to have their names placed on the lists of nominees; and for more liberal rules governing the scheduling of speeches from the floor. Not only did these proposals uniformly fail (sometimes because Gorbachev unilaterally ruled them out, sometimes because of lopsided votes against them), but the Moscow delegation's attempt to lead by example backfired badly. For the 29 seats apportioned to them on the Supreme Soviet's Council of the Union, the Muscovites nominated 55 of their number.[14]  The majority in the Congress leapt at this opportunity to defeat the more prominent democratic candidates on the Moscow slate.  Within the Russian delegation, to which eleven seats were apportioned on the Supreme Soviet's Council of Nationalities, the Muscovites again insisted on the competitive principle. Consequently, twelve candidates were put forward, thus leaving it to the full Congress to decide which one of the twelve would not enter the Supreme Soviet. The Congress chose Boris El'tsin.

This produced an institutional crisis. The spectacle of El'tsin, who had received by far the largest number of popular votes in the March elections, being denied a seat on the Supreme Soviet was a heavy blow to Gorbachev's efforts to build legitimacy for the new legislature. Fortunately for those concerned, a solution was found when one of those elected from the Russian Republic, A. I. Kazannik, voluntarily relinquished his seat in order for El'tsin to enter the Supreme Soviet.[15]  But the overall result of the experience of these elections and the way in which they were stage-managed by the apparatus led to another event of even greater moment.

On the day after the elections to the Supreme Soviet, a number of the radical-democratic deputies in the Moscow delegation (Yu. N. Afanas'ev, G. Kh. Popov and A. M. Adamovich) took the floor to announce that they and their colleagues had concluded that it was futile to continue to work constructively within the framework of the Congress as it currently existed. The apparatus, apparently avenging themselves for the humiliations suffered by many of their number in the recent elections, had been systematically obstructing the efforts of the Moscow radicals to prepare and distribute their own materials to the full complement of deputies at the Congress. Given the way that the apparatus had designed the procedures under which the Congress was working, and how it was using them to steamroller attempts within those delegations that it controlled to put forth alternative viewpoints and candidates, they argued that the time had come to organize an independent group of deputies who were committed to advancing the cause of democracy. Thus was born the Inter-Regional Deputies' Group.[16]

It seems quite probable that the decision to set up an organized opposition (in all but name) within the legislature was prompted in part by the enthusiastic crowds that were turning out after Congress recessed each day to rally behind the deputies of the democratic left. On the grounds of the sports complex, Luzhniki, which had been set aside for public demonstrations during the session of the Congress by the Moscow City Soviet, large gatherings of citizens, as many as 70,000 on one occasion, were assembling daily to cheer on the democratic forces.[17] Voters' clubs, organized in a number of the Moscow districts, enabled deputies to confer with their constituents during the evenings,[18] and further reinforced the impetus from below to engage the apparatus in open political conflict.

Denied printing facilities and a hall in which to meet by the President of the Supreme Soviet, organizers of the Inter-Regional Deputies' Group finally managed to hold a general meeting on 29 and 30 July in the auditorium of the Cinematographers' Union, relying on the Kurchatov Atomic Energy Institute for the printing of a draft programme and a newspaper, *Narodnyi deputat* (*People's Deputy*).[19] The 260 deputies who joined the Group on this occasion (their number grew, however, to nearly 400 within a few weeks) adopted a programme calling for a full transfer of political power to the soviets, repeal of those provisions of the Soviet Constitution that codify the Communist Party's political monopoly, a market economy and a free press.[20] A 25-member coordinating committee was also elected, led by five co-chairmen: Boris El'tsin, Viktor Palm of the Popular Front of Estonia and three veterans of Moskovskaya tribuna, Yu. N. Afanas'ev, G. Kh. Popov and A. D. Sakharov. Palm represented a liaison with the democratic movement in the Baltic, leaders of which formally declined to join the new group but expressed their support and their intention to cooperate with it in future.[21]

From the point of view of the grand compromise that underlay the entire process of democratization and the contending parties that it encompassed, the Congress of People's Deputies can be regarded as another round in the struggle between the apparatus and the democratic forces. The apparatus utilized the institutional machinery of the Congress to contain democracy and retain their grip on power, just as they had employed the various filters in the electoral system during the campaigns. In one sense, at least, they succeeded. The majority that they controlled in the Congress checked essentially every initiative put forward by their democratically oriented opponents. The apparatus thus held on to organizational power within the new legislative institutions, though these same institutions compelled them to exercise that power in a new way; namely, in the face of open and trenchant criticism from the democratic forces and, perhaps even more importantly, before the eyes of the entire nation. Survey research has shown that some 95 per cent of the Soviet adult population watched either all or part of the proceedings of the Congress on live television.[22] A majority of the respondents (63 per cent) in a subsequent poll reported that they regarded the apparatus as the dominant influence on what occurred at the Congress; 46 per cent of them said that this influence was a negative one, while 36 per cent evaluated it positively.[23] Although still outnumbered, the democratic forces were now fighting on more favourable terrain. They were developing their own bases of power by drawing larger and larger sections of the population into the struggle. As Boris El'tsin remarked shortly after the founding meeting of the Inter-Regional Deputies' Group:

> We are receiving heaps of letters and telegrams with serious and well-substantiated arguments in our support. Every week I meet with my constituents. Thousands of people have come to see me at industrial enterprises and institutes. Every time I get 300 to 400 written questions and notes. Not a single one has so far been negative with respect to the idea of our group. People write that it is right, and see it as Soviet pluralism in action, on the basis of which we ought to develop our laws.[24]

If palpable public support contributed to the decision to organize a visible democratic opposition, the very visibility of this opposition in turn served as a stimulus for organization and action below. A clear illustration of this process occurred in Kiev where a mass meeting with the deputies elected from districts in the city turned into a verbal brawl.[25] Registering their displeasure with the behaviour of their representatives at the Congress, those in attendance demanded to know why the Ukrainian deputies had not supported the democratic forces, why they had not called for autonomy for their republic along the lines of the Baltic model and why, after their 'dismal' performances at the Congress, V. A. Masol (Chairperson of the Ukrainian Council of Ministers) and V. S. Shevchenko (President of the Ukrainian Supreme Soviet) would not resign. Numerous speakers also demanded that the electoral system be thoroughly reorganized along democratic lines, a demand that gathered enormous momentum in the Ukraine over the summer of 1989 when the authorities unveiled drafts of a new law on elections and amendments to the Republic's Constitution. As we see, below, the 38 Ukrainian deputies who belong to the Inter-Regional Deputies' Group mounted a successful challenge to the Republic's authorities on this issue. Many of these same deputies have been in the forefront of a mass movement that has staged rallies in most of the Republic's major cities,[26] and a number of them have emerged as leaders of the Ukrainian popular front, Rukh, that was formally founded at summer's end.[27] In this respect, the democratic forces have taken on the double task of directing Rukh's activities toward an expansion of democracy within the Republic, while at the same time combatting the unsightly manifestations of chauvinism that have surfaced within Rukh.[28]

For all the limitations and filters that were built into the design of the USSR's new legislative institutions, this combination of a sizable minority of active and visible representatives with a growing democratic movement at the grassroots has substantially altered the political context in which these institutions function and, in so doing, has propelled their development in the direction of a genuine legislature. To date, this is most evident in the performance of the Supreme Soviet. Here, we briefly consider two aspects of this development, the Supreme Soviet's role in overseeing the executive branch of government and its participation in the legislative process.

*Legislative Oversight.* The selection of the USSR's Council of Ministers evinced some extraordinary institutional vitality on the part of the Supreme Soviet. In contrast to the longstanding pattern of blanket endorsement for the appointments made to ministerial and state committee posts by the authorities, the experience of legislative confirmation for these high governmental positions this time around was altogether novel. The Supreme Soviet rejected ten of the 70-odd nominees placed before it by Prime Minister N. I. Ryzhkov[29] and forced the authorities to bargain with the legislators and to compromise with them on some important issues.

The screening of nominees got under way on 19 June, shortly after the task of committee assignment had been completed within the Supreme Soviet.[30] The relevant committees (from among the fourteen formed in the full legislature) and commissions (four of which were formed in each of the two chambers)[31] then began their initial reviews of Ryzhkov's candidates. The early rounds of hearings, lacking 'fixed procedural rules',[32] were far from paragons of parliamentary behaviour. Nonetheless, they stood out as a definite advance in the direction of parliamentary government as many deputies, often catching the nominees unprepared, took the opportunity to interrogate them closely on matters of policy, administration, proposed budgetary allocations, and their own past performances in office.[33] When committee recommendations went forward to the full Supreme Soviet where the final votes on appointments took place, a number of Ryzhkov's candidates were voted down. The list of those rejected even included V. M. Kamentsev who had been nominated to the post of deputy prime minister.[34]

In the face of these rather stunning setbacks, Ryzhkov began to cultivate the political virtues of consultation and compromise with the legislature. Accordingly, he withdrew a number of the candidates that he had initially proposed after conferring with the relevant commissions and committees,[35] discussing with them in at least a few cases alternative nominations that would be acceptable to them.[36]

The issues raised most forcefully by the deputies during their deliberations on governmental appointments concerned ecology[37] and the civil and political rights of the population.[38] In the latter case, important ground seems to have been broken with respect to establishing and enforcing on the KGB a measure of responsibility before the people's representatives. This matter had already surfaced during the session of the Congress in an impassioned and sharply critical address from the floor by Yu. P. Vlasov of the Moscow group who referred to the security organs as an 'underground empire' responsible for the violent repressions of the past and constituting a menacing presence in the political life of Soviet society today.[39] It came up again during the Supreme Soviet's deliberations on the candidate selected to head the KGB, V. A. Kryuchkov. Certain deputies from the Baltic republics now complained about the unduly secretive activity of the security organs inside the country, and castigated them for their interventions against candidates opposed by the local apparatus during the recent election campaigns.[40] These unprecedented criticisms by the deputies led to some equally unprecedented assurances by Kryuchkov that hereafter a new relationship would be established between the KGB and the legislature, one characterized by *glasnost'* and real legislative oversight.[41]

*Legislative Function.* In its first session, which lasted less than two months, the Supreme Soviet either passed or initiated legislation on a broad range of topics: reforms in agriculture and industry that awarded important rights to firms and to the direct producers themselves; legislation on industrial disputes, military service, tax rates and assistance to the poorest sectors of the population; resolutions on fighting crime and corruption, on ensuring the political and civil rights of citizens, and more.[42] There has been considerable dispute, however, about the degree to which this legislative output has been the product of the deputies' efforts as opposed to that of the apparatus. Georgii Shakhnazarov, Chairperson of the Supreme Soviet's Subcommittee on Constitutional Legislation, has maintained 'that the main work is [now] done by the legislators directly' and to support his argument has cited as examples the draft laws on the press and that on unofficial public organizations, which were each authored by deputies.[43]

Other participants and observers, however, have been less sanguine. One issue here concerns the accessibility of those resources required for effective participation in the legislative process. The staff of the Prezidium of the Supreme Soviet and that of the Council of Ministers maintain offices either in or near the Supreme Soviet itself. Supplied with relevant materials, printing facilities, and a goodly number of specialists, these functionaries have remained the source of most bills coming before the legislature.[44] The deputies themselves have had to travel between the Supreme Soviet and their assigned offices located about a mile away in the New Arbat, offices that were still under construction during the first session. Many deputies have forcefully criticized this arrangement and, on not a few occasions, have demanded that clear procedures for formulating legislative acts be adopted along with broad publicity regarding their authors and sponsors.[45]

For our purposes, certain policy issues taken up by the Supreme Soviet during its first session merit particular attention. One of these, concerning the devolution of power to the republics and to soviets at the local level, is considered below. Here, we examine the response of the Supreme Soviet to two critical questions that confronted it; first, restrictions on the political rights and the civil liberties of the citizenry that were introduced by the authorities just prior to the opening of the

Congress of People's Deputies; and, second, the nationwide strike
conducted by miners while the Supreme Soviet was in session.

On 8 April, the outgoing Prezidium of the Supreme Soviet enacted
a decree concerning permitted speech that removed previous prohibi-
tions relating to so-called 'anti-Soviet agitation and propaganda' from
the criminal code and substituted in their stead sanctions against 'public
calls to overthrow the Soviet state and social order or to change it by
unconstitutional means'. However, the sections of this decree that
attracted the most attention were those which prohibited 'public insults
or discreditation of the higher organs of state power' or of those in
charge of them. This provision was regarded by some as revenge taken
by the apparatus for the criticism that they had endured during the
election campaigns[46] and interpreted by others as making all criticism
of government or party officials, however justified, subject to penalty.[47]
The wording of the decree was imprecise enough to sustain a range of
readings, and various legal specialists disagreed dramatically on the
issue of what it actually signified.[48]  In the face of widespread popular
reaction to the decree, the Supreme Court of the USSR issued a
'clarification' which stated that it should not be interpreted to mean that
citizens would now face criminal penalties for criticizing the state.[49]
But many remained apprehensive. Indeed, a number of deputies spoke
out vigourously against the decree both in the Congress and in the
Supreme Soviet.[50] Ultimately, the authorities backed down[51] and, in
consultation with the Supreme Soviet's Committee on Legislation,
Legality and the Legal Order, removed the offending sections on 'public
insults or discreditation' from the version ratified by the Supreme
Soviet at the close of its session.[52]

While this legal issue was being resolved in the committee rooms of
the Supreme Soviet, a wave of strikes engulfed the Soviet coal industry,
closing down mining operations across the entire country. Deteriorat-
ing living conditions seem to have provided the immediate material
impetus for this industrial action, the largest in the USSR since the
1920s. Although a discussion of these events is beyond the scope of
the present study, two aspects of the miners' strike are directly related
to our concerns. First, the Soviet working class was by no means
oblivious to the political reawakening of Soviet society that had accompanied the process of democratization. Not only did the altered political
climate, by changing perceptions of what was indeed possible, contribute to the decision to strike, but miners in a number of areas raised

decidedly political demands alongside the more conventional economic issues related to pay, working conditions and the provision of consumer goods.[53] Important in the longer term was the emergence of a grassroots movement of miners aimed in some instances at establishing either democratic control over their torpid unions or, in others, at organizing new unions outside the state-provided structures.[54]

Second, the miners' strike was something of a test for the new legislative institutions. Although the strike was brought to a successful conclusion through negotiations between representatives from the strike committees and their opposite numbers in the USSR's Council of Ministers, the Supreme Soviet played a role as well. Debates in the legislature, featuring many deputies from mining districts who shuttled back and forth between Moscow and meetings with their constituents, highlighted the legitimate grievances of the strikers and helped to tilt the political balance in favour of the workers.[55] Moreover, a number of deputies capitalized on the strike, arguing on the basis of direct evidence that here was proof that intolerable conditions were becoming even worse and that the long-discussed plans to restructure the federal system and devolve real power to local governments must now be translated into immediate action in these areas.[56]

## SOVIET POWER AT THE REPUBLIC LEVEL

Broad-based, popular movements in Estonia, Latvia and Lithuania have radically transformed the political climate in the Baltic and spearheaded the effort to realize soviet power at the republic level. We have already noted the role of the Estonian leadership during and after the nationwide assessment of the Constitutional amendments in resisting what they regarded as infringements on the rights of their republic by amending their own Constitution so as to nullify those features of the new all-union legislation that they considered to be in violation of their sovereignty. Developments in Lithuania followed a similar course. There, the popular movement, Sajudis, succeeded in initiating a new Constitutional project in that republic's Supreme Soviet that was published in draft form on 28 February 1989.[57] As in the Estonian case, the conception of federalism underlying the draft of the new Lithuanian Constitution was grounded on the idea of sovereign republics united by the imperative of common defence and the need to conduct a unified foreign policy, while voluntarily cooperating with one another on all other matters.[58] Consequently, the draft document, like its Estonian forerunner, regarded as null and void in the Republic any law or act of the all-union authorities not ratified by the Lithuanian Supreme Soviet. In recognition of the fact that this provision would itself contradict the Soviet Constitution, the Lithuanian authorities, in a move that perhaps showed more gall than deference, petitioned the Prezidium of the Supreme Soviet of the USSR to remove this contradiction by introducing appropriate changes into the all-union Constitution.[59]

A few days prior to the convocation of the Congress of People's Deputies in Moscow, the Lithuanian Supreme Soviet unanimously adopted its new Constitution.[60] The deputies acted immediately on its provisions by nullifying in the Republic a recent decree of the Prezidium of the Supreme Soviet of the USSR that established a nationwide highway tax whose revenues would be used primarily for road improvements in the less developed republics. They also took the opportunity to declare Lithuania's ultimate goal—to recover its independence.[61]

The delegations from the Baltic republics to the Congress of People's Deputies were quite unlike those from other parts of the USSR. Each contained a majority of deputies who were members of their respective popular fronts (in the Lithuanian case, 36 of the 42 deputies elected in that republic), and each was organized around a specific programme for national autonomy, expressed in the shibboleth, 'republic cost-accounting' (*respublikanskii khozraschet*). The leader of the Lithuanian Communist Party, Al'girdas Brazauskas, summed up the general orientation of the deputies from the Baltic on the relationship of republic cost-accounting to their aspirations for national self-determination. In Lithuania, he noted, economic initiative has been paralysed by the institution of all-union property which has enabled the authorities in Moscow to control some 90 per cent of the Republic's economy. The central ministries, behaving as *de facto* absentee owners, have time and again quashed attempts within the Republic to bring order to the economic chaos that has prevailed there. Although the entire country has been scheduled to adopt the system of republic cost-accounting at the beginning of 1991, he voiced the consensus of the leadership in the Baltic by insisting that 'in the face of the present situation in [our] republic, we cannot wait that long'.[62]

The question of republic cost-accounting was one of the most contentious issues taken up at the first session of the Supreme Soviet of the USSR. Of course, everyone proclaimed his support for the idea; it had been official policy of the Communist Party for well over a year. The real issue here concerned the matter of just how 'republic cost-accounting' was to be interpreted. Reform economist and newly-elected Deputy Chairperson of the Council of Ministers of the USSR, L. I. Abalkin, spoke warmly of republic cost-accounting during his confirmation hearings and mentioned the Baltic republics in particular as leading the way in this regard. However, he defined the concept in its minimalist version, specifying that extractive industries and the producers' goods sector would remain all-union property and, therefore, under the direction of the central ministries. His remarks were immediately followed by a short speech from a Lithuanian deputy, K. D. Prunskene, in which she reminded Abalkin that his conception fell far short of what the Baltic republics had in mind. Republic cost-accounting, in their view, would encompass the entire economic complex of each republic. In this 'maximalist' version, the central authorities could only influence economic behaviour in an indirect way by regulating a national market composed of republics, each of which would be in full control of its own economy.[63]

Toward the end of its first session, deputies from the Baltic introduced legislation into the Supreme Soviet of the USSR that would ratify at the national level the maximalist version of republic cost-accounting that had already been passed into law in each of the three republics. G. S. Tarazevich, formerly President of the Prezidium of the Belorussian Supreme Soviet, led the opposition to this proposal as he had with respect to Estonia's efforts to modify or postpone the amendments to the Soviet Constitution during the previous autumn.[64] Tarazevich's tactics were two-fold. On the one hand, he attacked the Baltic version of republic cost-accounting as unmindful of the economic injury that it would inflict on the rest of the country. On the other, he and his colleagues in Belorussia had already been busily preparing their own, far less ambitious, variant of republic cost-accounting as an alternative to the Baltic version.[65] On this occasion, however, the conservatives found themselves in a minority, and a very small one at that, mustering only 15 votes against the Baltic proposals.[66] An even stronger piece of legislation concerning economic autonomy for Estonia and Lithuania passed the Supreme Soviet as well. Under its provisions, the central ministries in Moscow would be required to cede title of all enterprises currently within their jurisdiction in Estonia and Lithuania to the governments of the respective republics by January 1990.[67] Future relations between the economies of these republics and the central authorities would be governed solely on the basis of formal contracts.[68]

The gains achieved by the Baltic republics in this respect doubtless stimulated movements for national autonomy in other of the constituent republics of the USSR[69] Yet for the Baltic republics themselves, uncertainty continues to surround the current situation. Although the Supreme Soviet of the USSR during its second session passed legislation establishing full economic autonomy for all three of these republics,[70] the intentions of the Estonians and Lithuanians to issue their own national currencies and permit private ownership of the means of production in small firms[71] would appear certain to test the limits of the compromise that has thus far been achieved. Compounding this economic question even further, however, is the tangled issue of political sovereignty.

The formal resolutions on national sovereignty adopted by the Estonian and Lithuanian supreme soviets have been followed by additional declarations that maintain that the annexation of these previously independent states by the USSR in 1940 was illegitimate and, ergo, lacks any legal force at present.[72] Although the Latvian Government has not yet taken this step, the same position has been formally espoused by the Latvian Popular Front.[73] As an indication of how far the movement toward sovereignty had come since autumn 1988, the provisions of a new draft law on elections in Estonia published in June of 1989 (abolishing the institutions of a Congress of People's Deputies and voters' pre-electoral district meetings in the Republic, as well as deleting the provisions of the Soviet Constitution regarding the appointment of deputies by public organizations) caused no stir at all.[74] It would appear that the political climate in the country had been fundamentally altered by the election campaign and the reaction of the public to the first Congress of People's Deputies. No one seemed willing to argue for the retention of these 'filters' once public discourse had passed the critical threshold where valid arguments must be authorized by principle rather than simply decreed by authority. Dismantling these filters, then, no longer seemed so radical a proposal. Indeed, as the union republics turned to the task of amending their respective constitutions and electoral laws in anticipation of local and republic elections scheduled for winter 1989-90, the filters contained in the all-union legislation were rejected in case after case.

The authorities in the Russian Republic deleted from their draft legislation both the idea of electing deputies in public organizations and the institution of the pre-electoral district meeting.[75] In the Ukraine, the legislative drafts prepared by the authorities not only replicated the anti-democratic features of the Soviet Constitution, but also introduced a provision guaranteeing seats in the legislature to certain 'distinguished candidates' (that is, the authorities themselves). Ukrainian members of the Inter-Regional Deputies' Group, however, spearheaded a groundswell of popular opposition to these proposals.[76] By the time that the Ukrainian Supreme Soviet convened in late October of 1989 to consider this legislation, the tide had clearly turned in favour of the democratic forces. None of the filters (pre-electoral district meetings, the selection of deputies by public organizations, reserved seats for distinguished candidates or the institution of the Congress of People's Deputies) survived the voting.[77] Moreover, an amendment from the floor was carried that would enable voters in local elections to choose directly the presidents of their respective soviets.[78] Events in Belorussia followed a similar course, although the resistance of the authorities to the demands of the democratic movement led by the Belorussian Popular Front was even stiffer.[79] Nonetheless, the Belorussian Supreme Soviet rejected all the conventional electoral filters, save that which concerns elections by public organizations. Here a comprise was reached, replacing the provision whereby one-third (120) of the deputies would be chosen by public organizations with one that set aside 50 seats for a select group of such organizations (Veterans of War and Labour, Society for Invalids, Society for the Deaf, and Society for the Blind) whose members were thought to be at a disadvantage in fielding candidates for general elections.[80]

Overall, these instances of constitutional change in the republics suggest that the arguments voiced less than a year earlier in the public debate on amendments to the Soviet Constitution had by now become the dominant tendencies in the country's political life. So much so, in fact, that the Gorbachev leadership was forced to resort to a blatantly unconstitutional manoeuvre simply to avoid the appearance that its Constitution of ten months was not being consigned by legislatures around the country to the museum of historical curiosities. Accordingly, the Prezidium in Moscow proposed to the Supreme Soviet that it vote to make optional what many of the republics were already deciding on their own (elections by public organizations, pre-electoral district meetings, the institution of the Congress),[81] although the Soviet Constitution clearly reserves such decisions to the Congress of People's Deputies of the USSR. Even this was not enough to stem the democratic tide, however, as the Supreme Soviet voted overwhelmingly (254 'yes', 85 'no') to amend further the Prezidium's proposals and abolish altogether elections by public organizations at all levels.[82]

But other aspects of the issue of republic sovereignty have remained explosive. A case in point was the provision in the same Estonian draft law on elections (referred to above) that established minimal residence requirements for voting and for holding elected office on all non-Estonians living in the Republic. This issue, unlike the other features of the draft law, could be joined by appeals to democratic principles. And those intent on putting the brakes on Estonia's movement toward full economic autonomy had by this time mastered the language of democracy well enough to do just that.

During the summer and autumn of 1988, a number of organizations (most prominently the International Movement, and the United Council of Labour Collectives) were formed in Estonia among Russian-speaking workers employed in large industrial firms under the direction of the central ministries. Their ostensible purpose was to defend the interests of national minorities in the Republic from the alleged nationalist excesses either perpetrated or contemplated by the Estonian Popular Front and their allies in the Estonian Communist Party. The available evidence suggests, however, that these were essentially paper organizations set up at the direction of the economic management of these large enterprises, probably with assistance if not encouragement from their superiors in Moscow.[83] The publication of Estonia's new draft law on elections provided them with the political issue they had been looking for. Here, they could argue, we see what the Popular Front and their supporters in the Estonian party and government have in mind when they speak of full national autonomy. They mean discrimination against non-Estonians.

Leaders of the groups opposed to the Estonian Popular Front organized a strike committee and issued instructions to the workers in their respective enterprises to lay down their tools.[84] Consequently, an openly 'political' strike, called by management, shut down a number of large enterprises and disrupted urban transport for weeks. At a minimum, this industrial action would guarantee that should economic power devolve to republic and lower-level soviets, as called for in the reform legislation, then those opposed to this plan from the beginning might still be able to command a sizable bloc of voters (the 40 per cent of non-Estonians residing in the Republic) and, thereby, remain in an influential position under the new conditions. At a maximum, this action might prove unsettling enough to sound yet another alarm about national animosities reaching boiling point and consequently persuade the deputies in Moscow to delay or even scuttle Estonia's plans for economic independence.

Within the Estonian Supreme Soviet, the issue was hotly debated over the summer months. After postponing a vote for some weeks and eventually offering some concessions to those opposed to the bill,[85] it was enacted into law on 8 August. Witin a few days, the Prezidium of the Supreme Soviet of the USSR struck down its provisions on residency requirements as violations of the Soviet Constitution.[86] Chastened yet again by a Declaration of the Central Committee of the CPSU published some ten days later in which the party leadership in the Baltic were taken to task for pursuing policies said to permit and even encourage a rupture in inter-ethnic relations while giving succour to 'extremist, separatist positions [of an] anti-socialist, anti-soviet character'[87], the Estonian authorities formally disavowed the residency restrictions that had been passed into law a few weeks earlier.[88]

The national question in the Baltic remains divisive and volatile. For the foreseeable future, a solution to it appears to depend on the institution of soviets. There are at least two reasons for this. First, the dicta of Moscow are no longer blindly endorsed by a political elite in the region whose careers depend primarily on the favour of the central authorities. As we observed during the nationwide assessment of the Constitutional amendments, the political leadership in each of the Baltic republics have struck roots in local soil, have entered into cooperative relations with the popular movement in their respective republics and have actively contested Moscow's policies on more than one occasion. Even in the face of the Central Committee's August Declaration, written in the suffocating prose of the pre-*perestroika* era (itself a signal that, after all, the clock might again be turned back), the party leadership in the Baltic, while conceding some errors, replied that the Central Committee was itself mistaken on a number of points.[89] The popular fronts in the region regarded the Declaration as 'impossible to agree with'[90] and even a 'provocation'[91] that some have initially responded to by stepping up efforts to expand national autonomy or, going even further, by organizing a movement aimed openly at secession from the USSR.[92]

This brings us to the second reason why soviets represent the political future of the Baltic republics. The political order currently prevailing in the region stands on two legs, the communist party and the popular front in each of the respective republics. The official renunciation of a 'leading role' for the communist party in the political life of Lithuania and Estonia, however, has opened the way for the development of multi-party systems whose outlines of this time are barely discernible. Yet it appears that the popular fronts there (and in Latvia, should that republic follow the same course) will splinter over time into hosts of separate parties, thus complicating considerably the political landscape. If these republics are to retain their membership in the Soviet federation in the face of strong internal pressures for secession, it would appear that soviets—in their capacities to respond to popular demands and to assume the role previously played by communist parties in integrating the individual republics into the larger political structure of the USSR— hold the key to this possible future. If, on the other hand, any of these republics does decide to leave the union, then a peaceful transition to independence would depend in large measure on its supreme soviet's ability to express authoritatively the aspirations of the public and negotiate with Moscow on this basis.

## AT THE LOCAL LEVEL

On 18 October 1989, the Supreme Soviet's Committee on the Work of the Soviets of People's Deputies presented to the full legislature a bill that proposed far-reaching changes in the area of local government. This bill had initially been formulated by the Council of Ministers and then sent to the Committee in July of 1989 where it subsequently underwent substantial revision.[93]   In late November of 1989, the Committee's draft appeared in the national press,[94]  thus initiating a nationwide assessment that apparently will conclude in spring of 1990. At the moment, then, it is impossible to predict the precise content of this legislation when it is ultimately passed into law by the Supreme Soviet or, perhaps, the Congress of People's Deputies at its spring 1990 session. Nonetheless, a review of this legislation's history allows us to reach some relatively firm conclusions on this score, at least with respect to the major dimensions of reform in the field of local government.

The new discourse of democracy launched at the Central Committee's January (1987) Plenum represented a decisive turning point for those concerned with the affairs of local soviets. As one legal specialist subsequently remarked, both scholars in the field and practitioners of soviet work had come to realize the futility of more 'cosmetic changes' (i.e., the legislation on local soviets that had been passed over the previous 30 years) and the imperative of undertaking radical measures. Indeed, he continued, the extant legislation in the area of local soviets has functioned as a 'brake' on their development.[95] In order to engage the real issues here, others added, a new type of language would be required. It is no wonder that the laws on local soviets had led to no practical improvements in their work. The inflated rhetoric of these would-be laws, their penchant for ambiguity and vague formulations, has reflected and, in turn, reinforced the impotence of local soviets.[96]

Soviets do not govern. Party committees, as we discussed above, manipulate their activity and this manipulation occurs within the context of the powerful centralized ministries whose enterprises, distributed on the territory of one or another soviet do largely as they please. Indeed, as one analyst has observed with perhaps a dash of hyperbole, it makes little sense even to speak of a city soviet, for there is in fact no 'city' for this soviet to govern; rather the actual content of an urban complex consists of a collection of settlements, each of which is attached to a large factory which is itself directly subordinate to some national ministry.[97] Such firms control the local economy and, thereby, determine the level at which goods and services are provided to the population. Obsessed with the fulfilment of central directives, the real masters of a given territory, the big enterprises, not only renege routinely on their own agreements to contribute resources to housing, health care, education and so forth,[98] but also manage to escape much or all of the tax burden for which they are responsible.[99] Deputies of local soviets, realizing that to speak out against this state of affairs is to invite 'subtle persecution' from the powers that be,[100] have passively endured the economic exploitation of their respective territories and the ecological ruin that has usually accompanied it.[101]

Some improvements in the work of local soviets have been recorded
during the early years of *perestroika*, with deputies taking a more active
part in the affairs of local government, and soviets themselves rising to
the defence of their respective populations to avert the harmful consequences of economic projects guided by the narrow self-interest of the
centralized ministries.[102] But the few bright spots in the overall, dismal
picture have tended merely to sharpen the contrast between what had
been accomplished in the exceptional case and what has remained the
rule for the overwhelming majority of local soviets. The need for
radical changes, introduced on a systematic basis, had become painfully
obvious. They got their start in Moscow in the form of empirical studies
that documented the chronic problems in this area and served as a basis
from which reformers in government and the academic world could
develop and argue for specific solutions.

The first of these studies was conducted in 1987, under the apparent
auspices of Boris El'tsin who served as First Secretary of the Moscow
Gorkom at the time. A research team composed of members of the
Institute of State and Law, the Institute of Sociological Research, and
the Organization Department of the Moscow City Soviet questioned a
random sample of some 616 deputies in the city about their work in
local government.[103] Not surprisingly, they learned that rank-and-file
deputies in the capital took little or no part in the work of their respective
soviets; indeed, even when they did attempt to represent the wishes of
their constituents in government, they found themselves helpless to do
so. Power at the local level was monopolized by party, soviet and
economic administrators. Among the implications that the research
team drew from their data was the necessity of building a real line of
responsibility between the deputies and the executive apparatus of their
soviets. Rather than proclaiming more paper powers for the deputies,
why not enable them to appoint the officials in charge of this apparatus
and thereby hold them responsible for their actions?

This line of reasoning was carried forward in the following year by
a second study conducted by the Methods Council of the Moscow City
Soviet. Here, the focus was on the interface between those who represent the public (the deputies) and those who dispense public services
(the administrative organs of local government). Concluding, again
without surprise, that the performance of both the representatives and
the public servants was grossly inadequate, this study proposed a
solution in the form of tightening the representative/public servant

nexus.[104] To this end, the organization, composition and activity of the standing commissions of local soviets would be thoroughly reworked. The longstanding practice by which the executive officers of soviets, acting on the recommendations of party committees and administrative bodies in the locale, assign deputies to standing commissions and designate their chairpersons would give way to one in which the full complement of deputies would decide how to distribute themselves among the commissions, while those elected to a given commission would in turn elect its chairperson. Freeing themselves thereby from the tutelage attendant on administrative appointments to these legislative organs, the standing commissions would be in a far better position to exercise real supervision over the administrative bodies that they are formally charged to monitor.

This focus on reforms in the structure of the standing commissions as a key to invigorating the institutions of local government led to another innovation—the creation of a directing organ in each local soviet, from district level on up, that would contain no senior administrators. Hitherto, the leading organs of local soviets, their executive committees, have functioned as extensions of administrative bodies organized at higher levels, a situation due in large part to the fact that those serving on executive committees have been in the main administrators appointed not by the soviet but by their counterparts higher up the administrative ladder. In order to break this administrative dominance in soviet affairs, the Resolutions adopted at the Nineteenth Party Conference called for the creation of a prezidium in each local soviet. Although nothing was stated in the Resolutions concerning the composition of these new bodies,[105] informed observers surmised that their membership would include the elected officers of soviets, including the chairpersons of their standing commissions.[106]

The working group formed in summer of 1988 under the auspices of the Prezidium of the Supreme Soviet of the USSR to draft new legislation on local soviets shared this same conception. Its members believed that by electing such a prezidium in each local soviet, the deputies, directly through their standing commissions and indirectly through the chairpersons of these commissions, would be able to oversee the administrative arms of their soviets, appointing, dismissing and thus holding accountable those in positions of administrative responsibility.[107] Designing a mechanism to implement this idea, however, proved a difficult and contentious task within the working group. As one of its members pointed out:

> [The draft law that we have been working on] states that the prezidium appoints and dismisses the heads of departments and administrations [of the soviet]. It seems to me that this is unnecessary. We must not forget that there are party organs that determine the *nomenklatura*, disciplinary actions and so forth.[108]

This issue, as well as a spate of other concerns expressed during its working sessions regarding the proper relationship between legislative and administrative bodies and what was indeed politically possible to introduce at the time, led the working group to eschew the task of drafting new legislation on local soviets themselves and to concentrate their attention on relations between the soviets and other actors in the local economy.[109] They succeeded in producing such a draft,[110] but it was never published and the working group itself was disbanded in February of 1989.[111] The main ideas formulated by the working group, however, were accepted and used as a point of departure first by a special committee of the Supreme Soviet that began meeting in March 1989 under the leadership of V. I. Vorotnikov, President of the Prezidium of the Supreme Soviet of the Russian Republic, and later by specialists in the Council of Ministers who prepared the draft submitted to the Supreme Soviet in July of that year.

The salient features of the legislation presently under public discussion include autonomous taxing powers for local soviets, complete with the right to lay rents on industrial firms situated on their territories.[112] Accordingly, local soviets will for the first time be in a position to form their own budgets and, therefore, to use their financial resources to address popular needs as they see fit. This will represent a considerable change. As a member of the initial working group remarked:

> Today's local soviet budgets are a parody of how to formulate a budget. They are not composed according to revenues but according to expenditures. It's not a budget. It means: 'You must build two polyclinics, three schools and five retail stores.' All that the soviet can do is say: 'We will build one of the polyclinics here and the other one over there'. They cannot do any more than that. What kind of local authority is that?[113]

As radical as the idea of real budgetary powers for local governments appears from the perspective of yesterday's practice, it has already (that is, before the new draft legislation has been made public) been attacked as a woefully inadequate remedy for the ills that plague local government. Instead, some critics would go further and sever the lines of authority that extend from the centralized ministries to the industrial firms that they direct. Rather than taxing these firms, soviets, principally at the regional level, would assume ownership over them, thereby placing control of the local economy directly in the hands of corresponding governmental institutions.[114] This scheme is reminiscent of the economic decentralization that was carried out during the Khrushchev period and resembles in certain respects the idea of republic *khozraschet*, discussed above. The draft legislation itself is unclear on the exact nature of future relations between local soviets and economic enterprises located on their respective territories. On the one hand, it includes provisions for the transfer of enterprises to local soviets and specifies that supreme soviets in the union- and autonomous-republics have the sole authority to establish the terms of transfer. At the same time, it seems to award broad regulatory rights to local soviets, stipulating that 'not a single question [involving] the use of natural resources [or] the construction or refurbishing of economic or social institutions can be decided without the agreement of the corresponding local soviet'. On the other hand, however, its implementing or enforcement mechanisms still contain elements of ambiguity that do not appear to favour the interests of local government. For example, local soviets are entitled to take polluters to court, but it is neither clear at the moment which courts would have jurisdiction in these maters, nor what penalties convicted polluters would face.

Whatever the content of the legislation when finally adopted, it appears likely that the resolution of the issue here will serve as a litmus test for the course of democratization in the immediate future. For at stake are basic questions concerning the distribution of economic and political power in the country. The transfer of property rights from the ministries to regional soviets would represent a fundamental change in the locus of economic decision-making. Economic power would devolve to the regions and the localities, thus enabling the soviets to assert themselves as the real 'masters of their territories' (to use the slogan that has accompanied their existence since they took power in 1917). But precisely to whom would it devolve and what conditions would structure its use? The many factors that bear upon an answer to this question are intertwined around the issue of political reform and, most especially, around the reform of the electoral system of local government.

At present, two radically different orientations are visible in the debate concerning reform of the electoral system of local soviets. The first one involves a further democratization of the existing procedures by removing the various 'filters' that now buffer relations between state and society. As we have seen, above, with respect to constitutional change in the republics, this tendency seems to be the dominant one at the moment. It might be described as 'liberal-democratic' since it proceeds from the idea of popular sovereignty and understands free elections, based upon the full political equality of all citizens (encapsulated in the term 'one man, one vote'), as the only legitimate means for constituting government. It represents the common political denominator among the contingent of radical-democratic deputies in the Congress and the Supreme Soviet, and enjoys the support of the majority of democratically inclined political groups in the country.[115]

The second orientation expresses itself in the traditional phraseology of Soviet democracy and leans heavily on the Leninist notion of soviets as 'working corporations' in which people's power is directly realized. From this perspective, the reforms advocated by the liberal-democratic forces would mean 'not people's power [*narodovlastie*], but administration of the people by the representatives of the people.'[116] In order to correct the flaws inherent in representative institutions and to ensure a direct role for the broad masses of people in the affairs of local government, advocates of this neo-Leninist orientation have called for the reintroduction (at the level of district and city soviets) of certain elements of the USSR's pre-1936 electoral system which privileged the category of work over that of residence and heavily weighted representation in favour of industrial workers. Under what is apparently the most popular variation on this approach, from one-third to two-thirds of the deputies of local soviets would be chosen directly on the factory floor of large enterprises in a ratio of one deputy for every thousand workers.[117] Gone would be the practice of public organizations naming deputies or the need to hold pre-electoral district meetings.[118] Its advocates contend that by basing the electoral system on 'large enterprises [which] are the only material foundation of socialism', this plan ensures that the new democratic forms of local government will have the proper 'socialist' content.[119] Although this tendency remains a minor one at the moment, its adherents have shown themselves influential enough to have their plan inserted into the newly-revised electoral provisions of the Russian Republic for some unspecified number of constituencies 'on an experimental basis'.[120]

On the surface, at least, it seems that each of these reform orientations envisages a different group of 'masters' who will be exercising, through their soviets, economic and political power in the localities. The liberal-democratic version focuses on the category of citizens in general, while the neo-Leninist one concentrates on workers in particular. Yet it would be naive simply to accept these categories at face value. If we were to ask in reference to the liberal-democratic orientation *which* citizens would be likely to play the major roles in politics were their proposals implemented, we would arrive at the conclusion that it would be those in possession of the requisite skills and resources (education, cultural capital, familiarity with the language of debate, and self-confidence in framing and defending arguments) —namely, the intelligentsia broadly defined. As such, we would equally expect this class to act on the basis of its own values and to institutionalize its form of life in the political order. Whether such would be a 'good' or 'bad' thing is beside the point here. Rather, we are only underscoring the tendency (which is readily apparent to their neo-Leninist critics[121]) of reformist intellectuals to couch their arguments and their interests in the language of universals, such as 'the citizens', when the actual distribution of the relevant resources in society would suggest that under their plan intellectuals themselves can be expected to appear as first among equals.

The particular interest embedded in the neo-Leninist approach is even more transparent. The plan for electing deputies to local soviets directly from the shop floor was born in Leningrad where the local apparatus was decimated at the polls in the March elections. Its leading organizational proponent, the Associated Front of Working People, very much resembles the self-described workers' and internationalist organizations cobbled together by the apparatus in the Baltic in opposition to the popular fronts there. Their proposals have been warmly endorsed by conservative party officials in Leningrad, the Ukraine and Belorussia,[122] but public opinion has so far tended to oppose them.[123] As their liberal-democratic critics are quick to point out, the scheme by which the deputies of local soviets would be elected in large factories is in fact a method by which factory administrators and party officials would control the composition of local governments. In the spring elections, the apparatus easily manipulated the nomination meetings in the great majority of labour collectives in order to ensure the selection of their preferred candidates and shut out all others; under the neo-Leninist proposal, they can be expected to do the same with respect to the election of the deputies themselves.[124] Critical commentaries aired in the Soviet press on this proposal have stressed the point that it has been 'planned by the conservative part of the party and state apparatus which is striving to get the forthcoming elections off the extremely politicized "streets and squares", and hold them safely under the protection of "fences and checkpoints" where ... the possibilities for manipulation are much greater'.[125]

Defining the shape of soviet power is at bottom, then, a struggle over the issue of who will exercise this power. More power to the soviets appears in every respect to represent the future of the USSR, yet how this future will unfold and precisely what forms it will assume are matters that remain governed by the contest for power. This struggle has characterized every stage of the democratization process and, as that process continues, we can expect that it will influence as well the alignments of the contending parties. The primary issue in the spring 1989 elections that knitted together a broad, albeit informal, coalition of democrats was a negative one: 'No' to the powers that be, 'no' to the apparatus. As *perestroika* has entered its second stage, however, the configuration of political forces has become considerably more complex. In part this is due to a backlash among those of conservative orientation who fear for their traditional values ('our socialist ideals') and are offended by those in the progressive camp who continue to shower their revered institutions with criticism. As one commentator has observed, the emergence of this element means that 'the authorities will receive more space for manoeuvre and in some cases will act in alliance with "democrats".'[126] At the same time, the increasing complexity and fluidity of politics are the necessary by-products of the transfer of real authority to soviets. As popularly-elected legislatures begin to assume power at all levels in the system, concrete questions related to practical matters will crowd the political agenda. This circumstance will likely fracture the democratic forces into groups with more or less specific orientations on programmatic goals. The same is true for the apparatus, or for at least those of its members intent on participating effectively in the new institutions of government and capable of adapting themselves to new political conditions. And as this process goes forward it will continue to transform the soviets from specimens alive only in the hothouse of the old regime's political mythology into institutions of popular government whose work in the world we can now begin to study and evaluate in practical terms.

## NOTES

1. A. Nazimova and V. Sheinis, 'Vybor sdelan', *Izvestiya* (6 May 1989).
2. 'Ob itogakh vyborov v Verkhovnyi Sovet SSSR odinnadtsatogo sozyva, sostoyav-shikhsya 4 marta 1984 g.', *Sovety narodnykh deputatov*, No. 4 (Apr., 1984), p. 5.
3. B. C. Gidaspov, Chairperson of the Mandate Commission of the Congress of People's Deputies, cited this figure in his report to the Congress, *Izvestiya* (26 May 1989).
4. Taking together the first and second secretaries in republic party organizations, and the first secretaries of *obkoms, kraikoms* and *gorkoms* of large cities, this group accounted for 12.1 and 7.6 per cent of the composition of the Supreme Soviet elected in 1984 and the Congress of People's Deputies, respectively. Nazimova and Sheinis, 'Vybor sdelan'.
5. N. Betaneli *et al.*, 'Mnenie deputatov...', *Izvestiya* (30 May 1989).
6. See, in particular, the comments made by E. Golikov, Deputy Head of the Ideology Department of the Central Committee of the Estonian Communist Party, in his Letter to the Editor, *Izvestiya* (23 May 1989).
7. See the interview given by Boris El'tsin to N. Selnorova and L. Novikova that appeared in *Argumenty i fakty*, No. 23 (10-16 Jun. 1989), p. 6.
8. For a similar analysis, see Viktor Kuvaldin, 'Deceptive Simplicity', *Moscow News*, No. 35 (3-10 Sept. 1989), p. 10.
9. See the remarks of Deputy K. A. Antanavichius delivered on the opening day of the Congress, *Izvestiya* (26 May 1989).
10. *Izvestiya* (26 May 1989).
11. Ann Sheehy, 'The Non-Russian Republics and the Congress of People's Deputies', *Radio Liberty Report on the USSR*, RL 270/89 (16 Jun. 1989), p. 22.
12. *Ibid.* See also A. N. Boiko's remarks before the Congress, *Izvestiya* (28 May 1989); and those of A. I. Kazannik interviewed by L. Novikova, 'Kak slovo nashe otzovetsya?', *Argumenty i fakty*, No. 24 (17-23 Jun. 1989), pp. 1-2.
13. See Yu. N. Afanas'ev's remarks to the Congress, *Izvestiya* (29 May 1989).
14. Only one other delegation, that from Sakhalin, followed suit, nominating two candidates for one seat on the Council of the Union. See the stenographic report on the third meeting of the Congress, *Izvestiya* (27 May 1989).
15. Since the vote for El'tsin was 1,185 in favour and 964 opposed, a procedure was worked out on the spot whereby the next candidate in line for a seat on the Supreme Soviet from a particular delegation would fill any vacancy that occurred in that delegation. See the stenographic account of the proceedings of the Congress in *Izvestiya* (31 May 1989).
16. See the stenographic account of the Congress in *Izvestiya* (29 May 1989).
17. Dawn Mann, 'El'tsin Rides a Political Roller Coaster', *Radio Liberty Report on the USSR*, RL 253/89 (1 Jun. 1989), p. 14.

18. Interview given by Yu. A. Belyakov to V. Azarnikova, 'Goryachaya tochka Moskvy', *Argumenty i fakty*, No. 23 (10-16 Jun. 1989), p. 3.

19. Andrei Romanov and Vladimir Shevelyov, 'The Minority Closes Ranks', *Moscow News*, No. 32 (13-20 Aug. 1989), p. 10.

20. Bill Keller, 'Soviet Congress Gets Dissident Bloc', *New York Times* (30 Jul. 1989).

21. 'Izbrano rukovodstvo oppozitsionnoi parlamentskoi gruppy v SSSR', *Novoe russkoe slovo* (1 Aug. 1989).

22. 'S"ezd glazami zritelei', *Izvestiya* (18 Aug. 1989).

23. T. Zaslavskaya and Ya. Kapelyush, 'Obshchestvennoe mnenie ob itogakh S"ezda', *Argumenty i fakty*, No. 26 (1-7 Jul. 1989), p. 1.

24. 'Why Should the Deputies Split?', *Moscow News*, No. 32 (13-20 Aug. 1989), p. 10.

25. See the eyewitness account of this event in David Marples, 'Angry Kievans Call for Resignation of Ukrainian Party Leaders', *Radio Liberty Report on the USSR*, RL 311/89 (2 Jul. 1989), pp. 20-22.

26. Valery Grishchuk *et al.*, 'To Elect or To Appoint?', *Moscow News*, No. 37 (17-24 Sept. 1989). pp. 8-9; Kathleen Mihalisko, 'Dispute in Ukraine over Draft Law on Elections to Republican Parliament', *Radio Liberty Report on the USSR*, RL 430/89 (6 Sept. 1989), pp. 21-24.

27. 'Rukh Starts on Its Road', *Moscow News*, No. 38 (24 Sept.-1 Oct. 1989), p. 2.

28. Nikolai Baklanov, 'Kommentarii RATAU', *Izvestiya* (15 Sept. 1989); Jonathan Steele,, 'Ukraine launches popular front', *Manchester Guardian Weekly* (17 Sept. 1989), p. 9.

29. Boris Nikolsky, 'We've Got a Government', *Moscow News*, No. 30 (30 Jul.-6 Aug. 1989), p. 8.

30. M. Kushtapin, 'Deputaty pristupayut k postoyannoi parlamentskoi rabote', *Izvestiya* (19 Jun. 1989).

31. A full roster of all these committees and commissions can be found in *Izvestiya* (13 Jul. 1989). The separate commissions formed in the two chambers of the Supreme Soviet were organized according to the respective areas of specialization and responsibility of the chambers themselves. Thus, for example, the Council of the Union has a Commission on Industry, Energy and Technology since these matters have national significance, while the Council of Nationalities houses the Commission on Nationalities Policy and Inter-Ethnic Relations. Some 800 deputies were assigned to the various committees and commissions, half of whom had been elected to the Supreme Soviet while the other half had not. This decision reflected the leadership's intention to expand the scope of legislative activity for those deputies who were not members of the Supreme Soviet by including them in its smaller working bodies as full-fledged participants. Additionally, the decision was taken to permit any other deputy to take part in the work of any committee or commission in an auxiliary capacity, equal in standing with the other members but without the right to cast a vote within it. See Kushtapin, 'Deputaty pristupayut...'.

32. V. Dolganov and A. Stepovoi, 'Kto voidet v pravitel'stvo?', *Izvestiya* (22 Jun. 1989).

33. *Ibid.*; V. Dolganov *et al.*, 'Proverka po vysshemu schetu', *Izvestiya* (24 Jun. 1989).

34. Andrei Romanov, 'You Might Not Be a Minister', *Moscow News*, No. 27 (9-16 Jul. 1989), p. 16; V. Dolganov *et al.*, 'Vakantnykh mest ostaetsya vse men'she', *Izvestiya* (4 Jul. 1989).

35. I. Abakumov *et al.*, 'Strogost' otbora, glubina analiza', *Izvestiya* (18 Jul. 1989).

36. See the comments of Evgenii Primakov, President of the Supreme Soviet's Council of the Union, in 'Learning to Hold Counsel', *Moscow News*, No. 34 (27 Aug.-3 Sept. 1989), p. 4.

37. E.g., Dolganov *et al.*, 'Vakantnykh mest ...'; Abakumov *et al.*, 'Strogost' otbora ...'; E. Gonzal'ez *et al.*, 'Zdorov'e naroda - zadacha gosudarstvennaya', *Izvestiya* (11 Jul. 1989); V. Dolganov *et al.*, 'Segodnya v tsene kompetentnost', *ibid.* (12 Jul. 1989). Perhaps as an indication of the importance attached to the ecological issue by the authorities, an importance brought home to them by both the deputies and public opinion at large, N. N. Vorontsov, a scientist with a long history of activism on environmental issues, was nominated and easily confirmed in the post of Chairperson of the State Committee for the Preservation of Nature. Of particular significance in this respect is the fact that Vorontsov is not a member of the Communist Party (in itself unprecedented for the holder of such an office) and is therefore independent of the party apparatus and whatever restrictions they might place on the holder of this post in order to curtail ecological vigilance and assist, thereby, their comrades in heavy industry who are notorious polluters.

38. E.g., A. Gronov *et al.*, 'Ekzamen na ministra', *Izvestiya* (23 Jun. 1989).

39. *Izvestiya* (2 Jun. 1989).

40. V. Dolganov and I. Korol'kov, 'KGB SSSR v svete glasnosti', *Izvestiya* (15 Jul. 1989).

41. Victor Yasmann, 'Supreme Soviet Committee to Oversee KGB', *Radio Liberty Report on the USSR*, RL 284/89 (20 Jun. 1989), pp. 11-13; E. Gonzal'ez, 'Formirovanie pravitel'stva zavershaetsya', *Izvestiya* (14 Jul. 1989).

42. A handy list of the legislative action taken at the first session can be found in 'Major legislation by Supreme Soviet', *Manchester Guardian Weekly* (13 Aug. 1989).

43. See his interview with D. Kazutin, 'Debate Gives Birth to New Laws', *Moscow News*. No. 38 (24 Sept.-1 Oct. 1989), p. 8.

44. V. Dolganov and R. Lynev, 'Sdelan vazhnyi shag', *Izvestiya* (7 Aug. 1989).

45. E. Gonzal'ez *et al.*, 'S"ezd i mir', *Izvestiya* (20 Jun. 1989); G. Alimov *et al.*, 'Formiruetsya pravitel'stvo', *ibid.* (27 Jun. 1989); V. Dolganov and M. Kushtapin, 'Debaty v pol'zu peremen', *ibid.* (20 Jul. 1989).

46. Interview with G. V. Barabashev (7 May 1989).

47. See, for instance, A. Churganov's Letter to the Editor, *Ogonek*, No. 21 (May, 1989), p. 6; Egidiyus Bichkauskas, 'A vdrug ispugaemsya?', *Soglasiya*, No. 6 (19 Apr. 1989), p. 1.

48. For a range of views extending from support for the decree as a 'great improvement', to criticism of its provisions as anti-democratic and simply 'wrong', see the following: V. N. Kudryavtsev, interviewed by V. Itkin, 'Demokratiyu okhranyaet zakon', *Sovetskaya Rossiya* (11 Apr. 1989); Aleksandr Yakovlev, 'Trudnosti zakonotvorchestvo', *Moskovskie novosti*, No. 16 (16-23 Apr. 1989), p. 1; A. V. Sakharov interviewed by Oleg Shcherbakov, 'I demokratiya imeet berega', *Stroitel'naya gazeta* (16 Apr. 1989).

49. Francis X. Clines, 'New Soviet Decree on Dissent Eased', *New York Times* (23 May 1989).

50. V. Dolganov *et al.*, 'Im stoyat' na strazhe zakona', *Izvestiya* (7 Jul. 1989).

51. Vice-President A. I. Luk'yanov, in his report to the Supreme Soviet, admitted that the decree was ambiguous and promised to amend it by incorporating the criticisms made at the Congress. 'Ob utverzhdenii ukazov Prezidiuma Verkhvnogo Soveta SSSR', *Izvestiya* (25 Jul. 1989).

52. V. Kurasov *et al.*, 'Prinimayutsya zakony', *Izvestiya* (1 Aug. 1989). The final version of the decree appeared *ibid.* (5 Aug. 1989).

53.  Kevin Klose, 'Soviet Workers Crossing Dividing Line Into Politics', *Manchester Guardian Weekly* (30 Jul. 1989), p. 17; 'Miners' demands reflect grim conditions', *ibid.*, pp. 7-8.

54.  David Remnick, 'A Proletarian Revolt—Or Just More Broken Promises?', *Manchester Guardian Weekly* (30 Jul. 1989), p. 18; Bill Keller, 'Soviet Miners Seek Control of Union', *New York Times* (17 Sept. 1989).

55.  V. Dolganov *et al.*, 'Deputaty ishchut reshenie', *Izvestiya* (24 Jul. 1989).

56.  G. Alimov *et al.*, 'Nuzhny konkretnye dela', *Izvestiya* (25 Jul. 1989). In the mining region of the Donbass, it appeared that the impetus given to these concerns by the labour movement forced the resignation of the president of the regional soviet. It also transformed the process of electing a successor from one in which the deputies listlessly approved the nominee of the party authorities into a lively contest among nine candidates decided by those ecological and social justice concerns that had been salient during the strike. See N. Lisovenko, 'Chetyre protsenta zaboty', *Izvestiya* (14 Sept. 1989).

57.  'Osnova pravovogo gosudarstva', *Vozrozhdenie*, No. 11 (17 Mar. 1989), p. 2.

58.  R. Stanislovaitis, 'Pochemu nam nuzhna novaya Konstitutsiya', *Sovetskaya Litva* (14 Apr. 1989).

59.  'Opublikovan proekt Konstitutsii', *Izvestiya* (1 Mar. 1989). By autumn of 1989, four union republics had added nullification clauses to their constitutuions: Estonia, Latvia, Lithuania and Azerbaidzhan. For details see the unsigned article 'O nesootvetstvii nekotorykh aktov soyuznykh respublik Konstitutsii SSSR', *ibid.* (13 Nov. 1989).

60.  'Sessii Verkhovnykh Sovetov soyuznykh respublik', *Izvestiya* (19 May 1989).

61.  Bill Keller, 'Lithuania Declares a Moscow Tax Law To Be Non-Binding', *New York Times* (25 May 1989).

62.  Al'girdas Brazauskas, interviewed by A. Radov, 'Razvyzhaem uzly nedoveriya', *Ogonek*, No. 24 (Jul., 1989), pp. 4-5, 28.

63.  Abalkin's and Prunskene's remarks on this issue can be found in I. Korol'kov *et al.*, 'Novoe pravitel'stvo: pervye naznacheniya', *Izvestiya* (29 Jun. 1989).

64.  I. Abakumov *et al.*, 'Verkhovnyi Sovet obsuzhdaet ukazy i zakony', *Izvestiya* (26 July 1989).

65.  This version of republic cost-accounting was approved for Belorussia by the USSR's Council of Ministers some six weeks later. Postanovlenie Soveta Ministrov SSR, 'O pervoocherednyky merakh po perekhodu Belorusskoi SSR s 1990 goda na novye usloviya khozyaistvovaniya na osnove samoupravleniya i samofinansirovaniya' *Izvestiya* (15 Sept. 1989).

66.  A. Davydov *et al.*, 'Pervyi shag k respublikanskomy khozraschetu', *Izvestiya* (27 July 1989).

67.  *Ibid.*

68.  Central Television, USSR, 'Vremya' (27 July 1989).

69.  In Moldavia, for instance, the national language has been adopted as the official language of state and the Latin alphabet has replaced Cyrillic orthography as its written medium. The session of the Moldavian Supreme Soviet at which these provisions were enacted was exceptionally spirited, owing to the intense opposition of deputies representing demands from the Slavic-speaking minority that their native languages, mainly Russina, retain a place in public life. Accordingly, a number of compromises appeared in the final version of the new law, making both Russian and Moldavian the recognized languages for communication among all national groups in the Republic, Moldavian the official language of business documentation, and leaving individual enterprises free to continue to use whichever language they had employed in the past for technical and work-related documentation. The utility of this

rather shaggy arrangement remains to be seen. But our point is simply to underscore the fact that a compromise among bitterly opposing factions on an issue as fundamental as this one was indeed reached within the Moldavian Supreme Soviet. On this subject, see S. Gamova, 'Put' k kompromisu', *Izvestiya* (1 Sept. 1989); 'Prinyaty zakony o yazyke', *ibid.* (2 Sept 1989). For a discussion of the genesis of similiar legislation in the Ukraine, see N. Baklanov, 'Proekt Zakona—na obsuzhdenie', *ibid.* (29 Aug. 1989); S. Tsikora, 'Mesyats na razmyshlenie', *ibid.* (6 Sept. 1989).

70. Zakon Soyuza Sovetskikh Sotsialisticheskikh Respublik, 'Ob ekonomicheskoi samostoyatel'nosti Litovskoi SSR, Latviiskoi SSR i Estonskoi SSR'. *Izvestiya* (2 Dec. 1989).
71. The Lithuanian version of economic autonomy, equivalent to that worked out by the popular fronts in both Estonia and Latvia, is set out in *Kontseptsiya ekonomicheskoi samostoyatel' nosti Litovskoi* SSR (Vilnius: Znanie, 1988).
72. See the coverage in *Izvestiya* (19 May 1989).
73. David Remnick, 'Baltic Nationalists Stand Firm Against Soviet Threats', *Manchester Guardian Weekly* (3 Sept. 1989).
74. 'Vyneseno na narodnoe obsuzhdenie', *Izvestiya* (27 Jun. 1989); Yuri Kraft, 'Should Democracy Be Egged On?', *Moscow News*, No. 32 (13-20 Aug. 1989), p. 9.
75. V. Dolganov, 'Vybory proidut po-novomu', *Izvestiya* (13 Aug. 1989); Alexander Obolensky *et al.*, 'Russian Federation, Ukraine, Byelorussia Pass Electoral Laws', *Moscow News*, No. 45 (12-19 Nov. 1989), p. 10.
76. Obolensky *et al.*, 'Russian Federation...'.
77. S. Tsikora, 'Sessii Verkhovnykh Sovetov soyuznyh respublik: Ukrainskaya SSR', *Izvestiya* (25 Oct. 1989); N. Baklanov and S. Tsikora, 'Sessii Verkhovnykh Sovetov soyuznykh respublik', *ibid.* (28 Oct. 1989).
78. Tsikora, *loc. cit., supra.*
79. See, for instance, the report of the President of the Belorussian Supreme Soviet, N. I. Dementei, to the legislative session considering the Constitutional changes in *Sovetskaya Belorussia* (27 Oct. 1989). See also a similar report by the First Secretary of the Communist Party of Belorussia, E. E. Sokolov, *ibid.* (28 Oct. 1989).
80. N. Matukovskii, 'Sessii Verkhovnykh Sovetov soyuznyh respublik: Belorusskaya SSR', *Izvestiya* (27 Oct. 1989). Texts of the Constitutional amendments, the Law on Republic Elections and the Law on Local Elections adopted in Belorussia can be found respectively in *Sovetskaya Belorussia* (4, 5 and 7 Nov. 1989).
81. A. I. Luk'yanov, 'Ob izmeneniyakh Konstitutsii SSSR po voprosam izbiratel'noi sistemy', *Izvestiya* (24 Oct. 1989).
82. A. Davydov *et al.*, 'Kakimi bydut vybory', *Izvestiya* (25 Oct. 1989).
83. See my 'Popular Fronts and "Informals"', *Detente*, No. 14 (1989), pp. 4-5.
84. Grant Gukasov, 'Mutual Wisdom and Flexibility Necessary', *Moscow News*, No. 35 (3-10 Sept. 1989), p. 9.
85. L. Levitskii, 'Estonskaya SSR', *Izvestiya* (25 Jul. 1989).
86. Ukaz Prezidiuma Verkhovnogo Soveta SSR, 'O nesootvetstvii Konstitutsii SSR nekotorykh polozhenii Zakona Estonskoi SSR "O vnesenii izmenenii i dopolnenii v Konstitutsii (Osnovoi Zakon) Estonskoi SSR" i Zakona Estonskoi SSR "O vyborakh v mestnye Sovety narodnykh deputatov Estonskoi SSR"', *Izvestiya* (17 Aug. 1989).
87. Zayavlenie TsK KPSS, 'O polozhenii v respublikakh Sovetskoi Pribaltiki', *Izvestiya* (27 Aug. 1989).
88. 'Plenum TsK Kompartii Estonii', *Izvestiya* (2 Sept. 1989).

89. The Central Committee of the Latvian Communist Party replied in part to the Declaration by noting that 'in many labour collectives and party organizations disagreement was expressed with the Declaration [because] it had not understood the unique developmental situation in each of the Baltic republics'. L. Litvinova, 'Obrashchenie Tsk Kompartii Latvii', *Izvestiya* (1 Sept. 1989).-
   The Central Committee of the Lithuanian Communist Party issued a communique following its meeting on the question that noted that the Declaration 'was not unanimously affirmed as has been the tradition', and complained that no member of the CPSU's Central Committee who works in Lithuania was involved in drafting the Declaration. Leonid Kapelyushnyi, 'Trudnyi poisk reshenii: Vil'nius', *ibid.* (29 Aug. 1989).
   In Estonia, a somewhat more conciliatory statement was issued by the Buro of the Party ('Obrashehenie Byuro Tsk ompartii Estonii', *ibid.* [30 Aug., 1989]), but the Secretary of the Prezidium of the Estonian Supreme Soviet was quoted in the national press as saying that the Declaration was 'untimely and not reflective of the real situation in the Republic'. Leonid Levitskii, 'Iskat' dorogu soobshcha: Tallin', *ibid.* (28 Aug. 1989).
90. Kapelyushnyi, 'Trudnyi poisk reshenii: Vil'nius'.
91. I. Litvinova, 'Trudnyi poisk reshenii; Riga', *Izvestiya* (29 Aug. 1989).
92. Michael Dobbs, 'Independence Movements Pose Major Challenge to Gorbachev', *Manchester Guardian Weekly* (3 Sept. 1989); Jonathan Steele, 'Hardliners gang up on Gorbachev', *ibid.* (10 Sept. 1989). In the Estonian instance, however, the Popular Front quickly took steps to lower the level of inter-ethnic tensions that had been mounting, explaining that further escalation was precisely what 'conservative forces in and outside Estonia' were attempting to promote in order to derail the Republic's steady progress toward autonomy. See Grant Gukasov, 'A Call for Political "Toloka" in Estonia', *Moscow News*, No. 38 (24 Sept. -1 Oct. 1989), p. 2.
93. See the report delivered by N. D. Pivovarov, Chairperson of the Supreme Soviet's Committee on the Work of the Soviets of People's Deputies, to a full meeting of the legislature in *Izvestiya* (22 Nov. 1989).
94. Zakon Soyuza Sovetskikh Sotsialistichesikh Respublik (proekt), 'Ob obshchikh nachalakh mestnogo samoupravleniya i mestnogo khozyaistva v SSSR', *Izvestiya* (22 Nov. 1989).
95. N. Starovoitov, 'Kompleksno i kardinal'no', *Sovety narodnykh deputatov*, No. 8 (Aug., 1989), pp. 11-12.
96. I. Butko and N. Selivon, 'Pravovye normy zhdut obnovleniya', *Sovety narodnykh deputatov*, No. 7 (Jul., 1988), pp. 18-21.
97. V. Parol', Urbanizatsiya i gorodskoe samoupravlenie', *Kommunist Estonii*, No. 1 (1989), pp. 43-54.
98. S. I. Shishkin has provided some startling figures to this effect, gathered in a study of the Irkutsk region that was conducted in 1984. Although three of the ministries of the Russian Republic had contracted with the regional soviet to allocate some five million roubles to the consumer economy in the region for that year, their actual spending in this areas was only 381,000 roubles. See his *Kraevoi, oblastnoi Sovet: Problemy kompleksnogo razvitiya territorii* (Irkutsk: Irkutsk University, 1988), pp. 75-76.
99. M. Alekseenko, D. Kisilev and R. Saranchuk, 'Kak povysit' dokhody byudzheta', *Sovety narodnykh deputatov*, No. 2 (Feb., 1988), pp. 33-88.
100. E. G. Andrushchenko, *Obshchestvennoe mnenie i glasnost' v sisteme upravleniya obshchestvom* (Moscow: Znanie, RSFSR, 1988), pp. 12, 35.
101. Shishkin, *Kraevoi, oblastnoi Sovet*, pp. 88-93; A. V. Moskalev, *Problemy sovershenstvovaniya mestnykh Sovetov narodnykh deputatov* (Sverdlovsk:

Uralskii University, 1988), pp. 78-86; Yu. Khrenov, *Chto mozhet Sovet?* (Moscow: Izvestiya, 1988), pp. 137-138.

102. *Inter alia*: M. Mirolevich, 'Ispolkom ne razreshaet pusk zavoda', *Izvestiya* (18 Apr. 1987); V. Buldashov, 'Deputaty rassmatryvayut kadrovye voprosy', *ibid.* (18 Jul. 1988); 'Sessiyu proveli deputaty', *ibid.* (8 Aug. 1988). See also in this context, Darrell Slider's discussion of the reform experiment conducted by the city soviet in Poti, Georgia, 'More Power to the Soviets? Reform and Local Government in the Soviet Union', *British Journal of Political Science*, Vol. 16 (Oct., 1986), pp. 495-511.

103. 'Sotsial'naya aktivnost' deputatov Moskovskogo gorodskogo i raionnykh v gorode Sovetov' (mimeo; Moscow: Moscow City Soviet, May, 1987).

104. G. Barabashev and E. Korenevskaya, 'Nauchno-Prakticheskie rekomendatsii po sovershenstvovaniyu deyatel'nosti postoyannykh komissii Moskovskogo gorodskogo i raionnykh v gorode Sovetov i ikh uchastiya v podgotovke reshenii Sovetov i ikh ispolnitel'nykh komitetov' (mimeo; Moscow: Moscow City Soviet, 1988); Yu. A. Prokof'ev, 'Rekomendatsii metodicheskogo Soveta pri ispolnitel'nom komitete Moskovskogo gorodskogo Soveta narodnykh deputatov po sovershenstvovaniyu organizatsii i deyatel'nosti postoyannykh komissii Moskovskogo gorodskogo i raionnykh v gorode Sovetov narodnykh deputatov' (mimeo; Moscow: Moscow City Soviet, 1988).

105. *19th All-Union Conference of the CPSU: Documents and Materials* (Moscow: Novosti, 1988), p. 132.

106. I. Il'inskii, 'Polnovlastie', *Sovety narodnykh deputatov*, No. 10 (Oct., 1988), p. 7.

107. Two members of the working group, G. V. Barabashev and E. I. Korenevskaya, emphasized this point during interviews conducted on 3 Oct. 1988 and 19 Oct. 1988, respectively. Another member of the working group, A. V. Luk'yanchikov who heads the Organization Department of the Moscow City Soviet, has discussed the idea at some length in his 'Postoyannye komissii i kadrovye voprosy', *Sovety narodnykh deputatov*, No. 4 (Apr., 1989), pp. 73-77.

108. These remarks of T. M. Shamba appeared in 'Stenogramma (obsuzhdeniya v GNK proekta Vremennogo polozheniya o predsedatele i prezidiume mestnogo Soveta narodnykh deputatov)', (mimeo; Moscow: Prezidium of Supreme Soviet of the USSR, 25 Oct. 1988), p. 28.

109. Report of G. V. Barabashev to the Kafedra of State Law and Soviet Construction, Moscow State University (16 Sept. 1988).

110. 'Proekt Zakona SSSR "O mestnom samoupravlenii i mestnom khozyaistve"' (typescript, 17 Oct. 1988).

111. Interview with Barabashev (7 May 1989).

112. A discussion of this issue can be found in G. Barabashev and K. Sheremet, 'Pravovaya baza obnovleniya mestnykh Sovetov', *Sovety narodnykh deputatov*, No. 9 (Sept., 1988), pp. 7-18.

113. Interview with A. V. Luk'yanchikov (14 Nov. 1988).

114. See N. Agafonov, P. Lebedev and M. Mezhevich, 'Vlast' na mestakh', *Izvestiya* (22 Aug. 1989).

115. For a concise statement of this orientation, see the interview given to Anatolii Golov by Yurii Boldyrev, a leading figure in Leningrad's Popular Front, who soundly defeated the head of that city's party committee, A. N. Gerasimov, in the March election, *Moscow News*, No. 34 (27 Aug.-3 Sept. 1989), p. 12.

116. Nikolai Travkin, 'Mestnaya vlast' dolzhna byt' dvukhpalatnoi', *Izvestiya* (26 Jul. 1989).

117.  A group in the Russian Republic, the 'Associated Front of Working People', has assumed the leadership of the movement advocating direct elections in the factories. Their affiliates and the outlines of their programme can be found in O. Shkaratan *et al.*, 'Za demokratiyu ili protiv nee?', *Izvestiya* (25 Oct. 1989).

118.  S. Troyan, 'Obsuzhdayutsya proekty zakonov', *Izvestiya* (22 Aug. 1989).

119.  See the interview given to Vladimir Kozhemyakin by Mikhail Popov, an instructor at Leningrad State University and originator of this scheme of representation, 'The Leningrad Experiment', *Moscow News*, No. 34 (27 Aug. - 3 Sept. 1989), p. 12.

120.  'Sessii Verkhovnykh Sovetov soyuznykh respublik: RSFSR', *Izvestiya* (28 Oct. 1989).

121.  Kozhemyakin interviewed by Popov, 'The Leningrad Experiment'.

122.  Troyan, 'Obsuzhdayutsya proekty zakonov'; Vera Tolz, 'Politics in Leningrad and the Creation of Two Popular Fronts', *Radio Liberty Report on the USSR*, RL 326/89 (5 Jul. 1989), pp. 38-40. In the Belorussian instance, see the remarks of V. I. Goncharik, head of the Belorussian Trade Union Council, to a meeting of representatives of labour collectives, 'Perestroika: rabochii sovet', *Sovetskaya Belorussiya* (30 Sept. 1989).

123.  A recent survey in Leningrad found that only 27 per cent of the public favoured the idea of electing deputies on the factory floor while 54 per cent opposed it. At the meeting in Belorussia mentioned in the note, above, a number of workers took the floor to criticize Goncharik's proposal as one advantageous to administrators rather than workers. The discussion appeared in 'Rabochii avangard perestroiki', *Sovetskaya Belorussiya* (6 Oct. 1989).

124.  See Boldyrev's remarks in his interview with Golov, *supra*.

125.  Quoted by Alexander Levikov, 'Are Leningraders Any Worse?, *Moscow News*, No. 32 (13-20 Aug. 1989), p. 10.

126.  Nina Belyayeva, 'A Review of Strength', *Moscow News* No. 49 (10-17 Dec. 1989), p. 4.

# INDEX

Abalkin, L. I., 141
Academy of Social Science, 43, 127; Scientific Research Institute of, 109, 148
Academy of Science, 96-7; Institute of State and Law in, 24, 147; President of, 94; Vice-President of, 96; Prezidium of, 96-7; Electoral Commission of, 97
Adamovich, Ales M., 62, 132
Afanas'ev, Yurii N., 62, 132-33
All-Union Council of Trade Unions, 93-4; Plenum of Central Committee of, 95
All-Union Society of Inventors: Central Council of, 95; Electoral Commission of, 95
All-Union Society of Philatelists, 93
All-Union Volunteer Society for the Struggle for Sobriety, 93
apparatus: of the party-state, viii-ix; of the Communist Party, 1, 3, 23, 35, 126; in the Congress of People's Deputies, 131-34; as reactionary, 25; as manipulative, 72-3, 91, 99-103, 107, 132-33, 154; in new conditions, 154: opposition to, 104, 107-10, 116, 137
Arbatov, Georgii, 95
Arkhangelsk, 100
Armenia, 105, 111
Associated Front of Working People, 153
Association of Cooperatives, 92
Avak'yan, S. A., ix

Baltic republics, 75-8, 104-05, 110-11, 113, 125-26, 129, 133-34, 136, 139-42; opposition to popular fronts, 144-45, 153
Barabashev, Georgii V., ix, 70-1

Belorussia 95, 113, 143, 153; Council of Ministers, First Deputy Chairperson of, 113; Automotive Works of, 113; Prezidium of Supreme Soviet, President of; 141; Popular Front of, 143; Supreme Soviet of, 143
Belous, N., 99-100
Boldyrev, Yurii, 112
Brakov, Evgenii, 112
Brateevo, 98
Brazauskas, Al'girdas, 140
Brezhnev, Leonid, 49
Burlatskii, Fedor, 50
Burtin, Yurii, 62

Caucasus, 103, 111
Central Asia, 103, 111
Central Committee of CPSU, 26, 43, 70, 80, 106, 108; January (1987) Plenum of, vii, 21-2, 36, 147; May (1988) Plenum of, 28; March (1989) Plenum of, 93; April (1989) Plenum of, 115; appartus of, 47-8; Propaganda Department of, 62; Theses of, 26-8, 44; electoral platform of, 108-09; subcommission of, 106; executive officers of, 126; Declaration of, 145
Central Electoral Commission, 6, 90-3, 97, 100, 102; Chairperson of, 90, 130; Secretary of, 90
Chebrikov, V. M., 77
Chepaitis, Virgilius, ix
Chief Arbiter of the USSR, 8, 10
Chudakov, M. F., x
Chulaki, M., 70-1, 73
Civic Dignity, 80
Collegium of State Arbitration, 8
Committee of Constitutional Oversight, 8, 10, 46, 74-5